BHUTAN

A KINGDOM IN THE SKY

BHUTAN
A KINGDOM IN THE SKY

M.S. KOHLI

IN COLLABORATION WITH
DEPARTMENT OF TOURISM
ROYAL GOVERNMENT OF BHUTAN

PHOTOGRAPHS
DUSHYANT PARASHER
M.S. KOHLI

VIKAS PUBLISHING HOUSE PVT LTD

VIKAS PUBLISHING HOUSE PVT LTD
576, Masjid Road, Jangpura, New Delhi-110 014
Phones: 24314605, 24315313 • Fax: 91-11-24310879
E-mail: helpline@vikaspublishing.com

First Floor, N.S. Bhawan, 4th Cross, 4th Main,
Gandhi Nagar, **Bangalore**-560 009 • Phone: 2281254

F-20, Nand Dham Industrial Estate, Marol,
Andheri (East), **Mumbai**-400 059 • Phones: 28502333, 28502324

35, Palm Avenue, **Kolkata**-700 019 • Phone: 22872575

C-8, 1st Floor, Nelson Chambers, 115, Nelson Manickam Road,
Aminjikarai, **Chennai**-600 029 • Phones: 23744547, 23746090

Distributors:
UBS PUBLISHERS' DISTRIBUTORS PVT LTD
5 Ansari Road, **New Delhi**-110 002
Phones: 23273601-04, 23266646 • Fax: 23276593, 23274261
E-mail: ubspd@ubspd.com • Internet: www.gobookshopping.com
• 10 First Main Road, Gandhi Nagar, **Bangalore**-560 009 • Ph: 2253903
• 60 Nelson Manickam Road, Aminjikarai, **Chennai**-600 029 • Ph: 23746222
• 8/1-B Chowringhee Lane, **Kolkata**-700 016 • Ph: 22521821, 22522910
• 5-A Rajendra Nagar, **Patna**-800 016 • Ph: 2672856, 2673973
• 143 M P Nagar, Zone I, **Bhopal**-462 011 • Ph: 5203183, 5203193
• No. 40/7940 Convent Road, **Ernakulam**-682 035 • Ph: 2353901, 2363905
• 2nd Floor, Apeejay Chambers, 5 Wallace Street, Fort, **Mumbai**-400 001 • Ph: 56376922

ISBN 81-259-1576-1

First Published 2004

Design: Dushyant Parasher

Processed and Printed by
International Print-O-Pac Limited, Okhla Industrial Area, Phase-1, New Delhi

PICTURE CREDITS

Dushyant Parasher
*Pages: 1, 2-3, 8-9, 10-11, 12-13, 18-19,
20-21, 25, 27, 29, 34, 42, 43, 44-45,
48-49, 50, 51, 52, 54, 55, 56, 57, 58, 59,
60-61, 67,68, 69, 70, 71, 72-73, 74-75,
76, 77, 78, 81, 83, 85, 86, 87, 88-89,
90-91, 92, 93, 94, 96, 97, 98-99, 100,
101(top), 102-103, 104, 105, 110, 111,
112, 114, 115, 116, 125 & Cover*

Captain M.S. Kohli
Pages: 33, 66, 120,127, 129, 135

Frank Hoppe
*Pages: 46-47, 80, 84, 114-115, 116,
117, 118-119, 137*

Bhutan Tourism
*Pages: 14-15, 16-17, 107, 108-109, 113,
138-139*

Dasho Jigme Tshultim
Pages: 62-63, 64, 65, 79

WWF Bhutan
Page 121

Courtesy H.E. Lyonpo Dago Tshering
Pages: 38, 39

End paper:
*Tashichö Dzong, Bhutan,
a drawing by Samuel Davis, 1783*

CONTENTS

ད་པལ་ལྡན་འབྲུག་གཞུང་།
བསྟན་རྒྱས་ལྷན་ཁག།

MINISTRY OF TRADE AND INDUSTRY
Royal Government of Bhutan
Tashichho Dzong
Thimphu

བསྟན་རྒྱས་བློན་པོ།
MINISTER

FOREWORD

After centuries of self-imposed isolation during which Bhutan remained virtually closed to the world outside, the first intrepid travellers began trickling into the country in 1974, following the coronation of the reigning monarch, King Jigme Singye Wangchuck. Some three decades later, the number of tourists coming to the country is still relatively small, with an average of around five to six thousand arrivals per annum, peaking at over seven thousand in 2001.

Bhutan chooses to remain an exclusive destination where the emphasis is on 'low volume, high value' tourism. This approach is in consonance with our development philosophy, which places high premium on Gross National Happiness (GNH). GNH rests on four pillars—the preservation of our cultural heritage, protection of our pristine environment, equitable socio-economic development and good governance. While this is not to claim that we hold the magic formula to ensure happiness for all, we believe that material progress is only one of other equally important components.

Captain M.S. Kohli has travelled extensively throughout the country and observed first hand how Bhutan has been trying to meet the forces of change and modernization on her own terms. He obviously likes what he sees—in the people, the government and the country. Trekking through virgin trails and pristine meadows of Bhutan nearly two decades ago, the yearning to record the fascinating sights to which he was privy nagged the mountain lover. He dreamed of bringing out a pictorial book on the country. His dream was realized when the Royal Government invited him back a few years ago. Accompanied by accomplished photographer Dushyant Parasher, Captain Kohli returned to Bhutan.

The result—A Kingdom in the Sky—is a welcome addition to the several books on Bhutan, which have been published during recent years. The relatively small population and the Royal Government's commitment to conservation makes the country one of the most unspoilt destinations on earth. The words and the pictures convey the myriad colours of wild flowers, trees in seasonal bloom and forests where exotic animals roam. Traditional architecture, the colourful people in their national costumes and their living culture, are lovingly portrayed in the book. Found in no other book, perhaps, is a brief description of the mountaineering aspect of Bhutan and this should come as no surprise, as Captain Kohli is a renowned climber himself.

I am positive this book will be of interest not only to those who have visited the country and would like to keep a memento, as well as those who are contemplating a trip to a unique destination, but also to others who are curious and would like an introduction to the Himalayan Kingdom called Bhutan.

Lyonpo Khandu Wangchuk

INTRODUCTION

Bhutan, to me, had remained an enigmatic and a far-off land for a very long time. For years, I conjured up mysterious visions of this country and year after year planned a trip, which somehow never materialised. In fact, Bhutan always remained in my thoughts when I was promoting the Himalayas during my Air-India days. I used to talk of not only Nepal, Pakistan and Tibet but also of Bhutan as all these countries share a rich Himalayan heritage. My love for all the Himalayan countries remained unabated, irrespective of the prevailing political scenarios.

The opportunity, and that too in a most interesting fashion, came my way in March 1984 when the World Tourism Organisation and the Royal Government of Bhutan invited me to visit the Himalayan kingdom to trek extensively and assist in drawing the adventure aspect of the Tourism Master Plan for Bhutan. The three months that I spent in Bhutan provided me with a rare opportunity of seeing the fascinating country and its beautiful people. Ever since then I had the desire to write a pictorial book on Bhutan. However, due to overwhelming pressure of work in my various Air-India assignments, I could not do so.

Seventeen years later, in April 2001, I had another opportunity to visit Bhutan. During this visit, in collaboration with the Royal Government of Bhutan, I decided to go ahead with my plans of bringing out an illustrated book on the unspoilt Himalayan kingdom. During this visit I was accompanied by Dushyant Parasher, a leading graphic designer and travel photographer. Photographs used in the book have been taken by both of us. But the illustrated part of this book would not have been complete without some excellent photographs from Frank Hoppe, Dasho Jigme Tshultim, H.E. Lyonpo Dago Tshering, WWF Bhutan and Bhutan Tourism.

During my first visit to Bhutan, I found that normally the Royal Government permitted tourists to visit only the western and central parts of the country, but happily, I was permitted to visit all parts of Bhutan to carry out a detailed survey. This was indeed a great opportunity. The eastern part of Bhutan, which touches Arunachal Pradesh in India, has a great wealth of flora and fauna. At present tourists are allowed to visit this area. On one particular trek I saw the greatest spectacle of my life, a thick forest of rhododendrons with multicoloured flowers blooming on both sides of the meadow that stretched for four or five kilometres. This was among the most enjoyable parts of my stay in Bhutan.

The virgin landscape of Bhutan, the unique architecture of its buildings in the form evolved centuries ago, and miles and miles of uninhabited terrain stood in sharp contrast to the crowded trekking trails in the neighbouring countries. The impressive and colourful *dzongs*, and the beauty of its people and their dresses which blended in perfect harmony with each other, left an everlasting impression on me.

Bhutan is a land of people who are never in a hurry, but are full of life. It is also a land of local festivals which go on throughout the year in different towns and villages. They are not only colourful and interesting but retain their authentic form that has not so far been affected by visitors.

Astrologers play an important role in the lives of the Bhutanese. It can take as long as one month before a body is cremated if the astrologer does not find a suitable day earlier than that. Astrologers also recommend the remedy and the appropriate prayer for curing sickness which is supposed to be the result of one's *karma*. Just as the *Shivling*, the phallic symbol, is worshipped by the Hindus in India, in Bhutan, it is painted and hung around for its protective powers. Such images are a common sight on top of most rural and sub-urban houses and buildings. It is believed that these symbols have protective powers. Archery is Bhutan's national sport. Anyone who hits the bull's eye is an instant celebrity and there is much merriment to celebrate the event.

While the majority of Bhutanese are farmers and lead simple lives in their villages, Bhutan also has a fair number of highly educated and sophisticated young persons who have studied in the West, particularly the USA. These dynamic, and forward-looking persons, no doubt, would play an important role in shaping the future of Bhutan. The Bhutanese king symbolises all the good qualities of the Bhutanese. He is also a great sportsman.

Having remained closed to the outside world for centuries, till recently, Bhutan was regarded as an exclusive and rare destination about which the mind of an average tourist, who had heard only a little about Bhutan, conjured up mysterious notions.

Bhutan opened its mountains to climbers for only a short period, from 1983 to 1994. As such the country's mountaineering history is correspondingly brief. Jhomolhari was climbed from Tibet in 1937 by F Spencer Chapman and a Sherpa, and again in 1970 by a joint Indian-Bhutanese team. A Bhutanese expedition scaled the 4,900 m Thurigang, north of Thimphu, in 1983. Jichu Drake was attempted three times before it was successfully climbed in 1988 by an expedition led by Dough Scott. Masang Gang was climbed by a Japanese expedition in 1985, and Gangkhar Puensum (7,541 m) remains the highest unclimbed peak in the world after unsuccessful attempts by Japanese and British teams in the 1980s.

CAPTAIN M.S. KOHLI

The Unspoiled Kingdom

Bhutan has many names, steeped in myths and traditions: Druk Yul—the Land of the Thunder Dragon (sometimes the Land of the Peaceful Thunder Dragon), Beyul—the Hidden Holy Land, Lhomon Khashi—the Southern Monpa Country of Four Approaches, to mention a few. Ancient chroniclers of Tibet referred to Bhutan as the Lotus Garden of the Gods. Bhutan has also been called Menjong—the Valley of Medicinal Herbs.

From as early as the seventh century, the tiny kingdom Druk Yul has existed as an independent nation. Awesome natural barriers and imposing mountain-ranges separate it from the hill districts of India in the east and west; towering in the north-east the stark mountains of the Jhomolhari range provide the frontier with the Chumbi Valley of Tibet. In the infinite wastes of ice and snow of the savage snow peaks of the great Himalayas lies the border with the Tibetan region of China.

Secluded from its neighbours by some of the highest mountain ranges in the world, Bhutan has only recently emerged from its self-imposed isolation. This country of uncommon customs, fascinating legends and scenery of breathtaking beauty remained a mythical Shangri-La for a long time. Early travellers marvelled at its inaccessibility, for they could reach the heart of the country only after days or weeks of arduous trekking. Now, however, from an isolated feudal state, Bhutan is slowly developing into a member of the world community; but for all the outward signs of modernity—new roads, schools, hospitals—it remains a profoundly traditional and religious society, retaining firmly its rich and valued heritage of the past.

Occupying an area of approximately 18,000 square miles, the far north of Bhutan lies in the great Himalayas, a sparsely inhabited area of giant snow peaks and glacial lakes. The bulk of the 600,000 population lives in the inner Himalayas at an altitude of 3,500 to 10,000 feet. The land here is extensively cultivated, and the high annual rainfall breeds luxuriant vegetation and dense forest.

The Bhutanese are a hardy, well-built people, skilled archers and industrious farmers. Despite their strong martial spirit they are peaceful and fun-loving. The people fall into three broad ethnic groups—the Scharchops, the Naglops and the Lhotsampas. The first of these, the Scharchops, are believed to have been the earliest inhabitants of the country and live largely in the eastern regions. Apparently Indo-Mongolian, their actual origin and ancestry remain a mystery. The Naglops, descendents of Tibetan immigrants who came to Bhutan in about the ninth century, settled primarily in the west. The third section of population, Lhotsampas (people of Nepali origin), began to settle in the southern region towards the end of the nineteenth century.

Bhutan today is only 45 minutes away by air from Kolkata. In less than an hour one could well be flying back in time into a dream world—the last Shangri-La. From the teeming, screaming and bustling eastern Indian metropolis one lands in a land of

A young Bhutanese girl enjoying a quite moment in eastern Bhutan.

serene calmness, breathtaking scenery, colourful and cheerful people, Buddhist temples and *dzongs* of eye-catching architecture and, above all, majestic mountains that embrace this tiny Himalayan kingdom. Within a span of about 200 kilometres one can see sub-tropical forests, the steep rise of the Himalayas and the perennially white peaks of snowy mountains.

The Bhutanese attire is among the first sights to arrest attention upon landing in the kingdom. Men move about in *gho* or *boku*, which is a long robe tied around the waist by a slim belt, *kera*. A small sword, slung or tucked at the waist, helps in chopping betel nuts, meat or wood. It is the sign of the egalitarian nature of the Bhutanese society that all men, from the king to the humblest, wear the same costume.

Likewise, all women wear ankle-length robe, *kira*, which is made from coloured, finely woven fabrics. Each valley has its own traditional pattern. Silver brooches–*koma*–fasten the *kira* at the shoulders while the *kera* holds it at the waist. The necklaces are made of coral, pearls, turquoises and precious agate eyestones which are called the *tears of God*.

But the most striking physical feature of Bhutan is its architecture, the aesthetically rich style and colour of its buildings and houses. The most outstanding buildings are the imposing *dzongs* of the 17th century which were built incredibly without any drawing. Rich colours adorn every wall, beam, pillar and door of Bhutanese buildings. No less impressive is the art and paintings which reflect the spiritual and artistic wealth of Bhutan. The colourful murals, *thangkhas*, are painted with vegetable dyes.

With so much of colour in their everyday life, it is only natural that religious festivals and dances are among the many attractions of Bhutan. These religious festivals, called *tshechus*, are celebrated to honour Guru Rinpoche and are occasions for prayers and blessings, feasting and socialising. Though these festivals are held the year round, two of the most popular ones are held at Paro in the spring and Thimpu during autumn.

The country has preserved its eco-diversity remarkably well. Its great diversity of plants and animals makes Bhutan one of the ten most important areas on earth for bio-diversity conservation. A large number of endangered species can be found in Bhutan because of the rich forests that cover nearly two-thirds of the country. In fact, Bhutan is one of the last remaining refuges for many species. It is also an ecological treasure trove. The Buddhist respect for life has ensured preservation of wildlife.

The moist climate in the eastern part promotes plant growth that provides varied habitats for animals. The manner in which the proud people of Bhutan have kept alive their ancient culture, art, crafts and traditions stands out in contrast with the damage

that many countries around the world have suffered in their blind pursuit of hedonistic pleasures. Perhaps, Bhutan has to thank God and Nature for its ability to retain its pristine and pure past.

Much of the kingdom is surrounded by the lofty and

Exotic ferns growing on a hillside

foreboding Himalayas, acting as a natural barrier against all invasions. The British, and before them the armies of Muslim invaders, could not set upon an adventure further north to grab the country of 46,000 square kilometres, about the size of Switzerland.

Bhutan is not only land-locked but it is also a unique staircase-shaped country that starts with a narrow lowland in the south, about 300 metres above the sea level, rising to the high Himalayan peaks of over 7000 metres in the north. In between lies the densely populated, jungle-covered central valley of deep gorges.

The kingdom of Bhutan is surrounded by the Tibet region of China to the north and the north-west and the Indian states of Assam, West Bengal and Sikkim on the other sides. Rich forests continue to cover the mountain slopes of Bhutan—a sign of how strict and careful the kingdom has been in guarding its rich forests through a programme of re-afforestation. Since the trees and the vegetation have been so well preserved, sufferings from natural disasters are not as common in Bhutan as in many other mountainous regions of the world.

There are three geographic—and climatic—zones in which the country can be divided. The foothills have a tropical climate. The inner Himalayan region has a temperate climate which receives monsoon rains. The high Himalayan region is Alpine in its severity. Interestingly, the people of today's Bhutan can also be classified into three groups. In the central region live people who are of Mongoloid origin, most of whom are cattle farmers. They live in small towns that have grown around *dzongs*, the fortified monasteries. The northern Himalayan zone is the haunt of the semi-nomadic yak herdsmen who live in tents woven from yak hair or dry-wall stone houses. The southern part is home to the *Lhotshampas*. Agriculture and cash crops are their main occupation.

The climatic variation contributes to Bhutan's immensely rich flora and fauna that has often found itself depicted in the extremely colourful and popular postage stamps of Bhutan. The fertile valleys of Bhutan produce a great variety of fruits and vegetables. Rice paddy is also grown extensively.

Before the border with Tibet, which is to the north of Bhutan, was closed in 1959, there was a brisk barter trade between the two neighbours in which animals were an important commodity.

Even while living in the safety of an idyllic Himalayan cocoon, most Bhutanese greet visitors warmly and seem contented with life. They are full of laughter, songs and dances. For generations, many of the 'ordinary' Bhutanese have lived in large exquisitely painted wooden houses with walls of dried mud. The quaint Bhutanese houses lend a colour of their own to the landscape.

Certain stone implements found in Bhutan suggest that the country was inhabited as far back as 2000 BC. But it cannot be said with authority as archeological research has not been Bhutan's strong point. Access to Bhutan was never easy, after all. For centuries the only visitors to Bhutan were the monks and lamas seeking refuge from the rigorous environments of their native land. The first westerners to land in Bhutan were said to be two Portugese Jesuit priests in 1627. In the next 300 years, only 13 European expeditions were known to have visited Bhutan.

The documented history of Bhutan begins in the eighth century when Guru Padmasambhava, an Indian tantric, arrived from Tibet in AD 747 on the back of a tigress. The Guru is believed to have visited Bhutan three or four times. He made his first visit to Bumthang from Nepal at the invitation of Sinthu Raja, the king of Bumthang. He was also known as Pemajungne, or Guru Rinpoche, and was considered by the old school of Bhutan as their spiritual master and the second Buddha. As he did in Tibet, he introduced a tantric strain of Mahayana Buddhism in Bhutan. The places he visited and meditated became places of pilgrimage for the Bhutanese who also worship his eight manifestations.

For two centuries after Guru Rinpoche alighted in the valley of Paro, Bhutan went into obscurity. There was turmoil in Tibet where Buddhism itself was in danger. Many Buddhist monks and saints fled to Bhutan.

A period of great revival of Buddhism began in Bhutan in the 11th century when Tertons, the Discoverers of Treasures, in Paro and Bumthang discovered texts hidden by Padmasambhava and other saints. In fact, the period between the 11th and the 17th centuries saw a great deal of Buddhist missionary activity in Bhutan, though the country also showed a lack of political unity.

The biggest religious expansion in the country was witnessed between the end of the 11th century and the beginning of the 12th century when a number of religious schools came into existence —Kadampa, Kagyupa and Sakyapa schools among them. In the 15th century, an interesting visitor who landed in western Bhutan was the wandering Drukpa Kunley who belonged to the princely family of Gya. Often referred to as the Divine Mad Man, every Bhutanese is familiar with his adventures. His method of teaching the essence of religion and songs was said to be 'eccentric' and his behaviour 'shocking'. While most of the Buddhist monks came to Bhutan from Tibet, especially from 14th century onwards, quite a few were native born. The most famous among them was Pema Lingpa, a descendant of Gyalwa Lhanangpa, a reincarnation of Guru Rinpoche, who also originated many sacred dances that appeared to him in a vision.

Bhutan, however, had to wait till the 17th century before emerging as a unified state. The credit goes to the charismatic Ngawang Namgyal of the Drukpa school who was a religious teacher with a political vision. He was also an able administrator. Taking the title of Zhabdrung—'At Whose Feet One Submits'— he had fled from Tibet to arrive in Bhutan in AD 1616. In Tibet, his recognition as the incarnation of the Drukpa scholar, Pema Karpo, was challenged by Tsang Desi, head of the Tsang province in Tibet.

He had to wage battles against his enemies in Tibet and in Bhutan; but he managed to give Bhutan a system of laws based on unwritten codes. He established a state monk body under a religious leader, the Je Khempo, and a theocracy administered by monks headed by a temporal leader, the Desi. This dual system of government was called *Choesi*. It needed time to be consolidated and the nation had to be saved from any further turmoil. That is why for nearly 50 years the death of the Zhabdrung had to be kept a secret.

The Zhabdrung had established an extensive system of laws and built a chain of *dzongs* to guard every valley. Now these *dzongs* serve as the religious and administrative centres of the region. But once again there were unsettled times in Bhutan. The dual system of government led to factional wars. Bhutan was caught in intermittent civil wars. It also had to ward off British

Ruins of Drugyel Dzong in Paro Valley

colonial ambitions. By the end of the 19th century, the central government had become markedly weak as two centres of power, the governors (*penlops*) of Paro and Trongsa, had de facto control of western and central Bhutan. The power struggle between the two governors was nearing its climax in 1904. The governor of Paro, influenced by China, decided to side with Tibet. The Trongsa *Penlop*, Ugyen Wangchuck, under advice from Kazi Ugyen Dorji, decided to cooperate with the British. Ugyen Wangchuck, overcame his rivals to unite the nation once again. On 17 December, 1907, he was unanimously elected as the first king of

Bhutan by a Constituent Assembly which had representatives of monks, civil servants and the people.

The dual system of government came to an end as Bhutan entered an era of hereditary monarchy which was further modified to incorporate democratic strains. Ugyen Wangchuck died in 1926. His son Jigme Wangchuck ruled till his death in 1952. The next king was Jigme Dorji Wangchuck whose eventful rule from 1952 to 1972 saw the country opening up to the outside world and embark on a course of economic and social development.

Busy in the fields near Punakha

The National Assembly was set up in 1953 with 150 members who included elected representatives as well as the clergy and government nominees. In 1971, a year before his end, Bhutan had become a member of the United Nations. Today,

Bhutan is ruled by his enlightened son, King Jigme Singye Wangchuck, who brought about the historic devolution of power by the formation of a Council of Ministers in 1998, with a great vision for the Nation. Bhutan has 20 administrative districts. The judiciary consists of lower courts and a high court at Thimpu, the capital. But Bhutanese can appeal to the king as a last resort. Bhutan embarked upon its economic development in 1961 through five-year plans. But a more daunting task it took quite successfully was to introduce the modern monetary economy in a country which had a long tradition of the barter system of trade. Almost 95 per cent of the Bhutanese earn their livelihood from farming and cattle-breeding. There is also a growing small-scale industry in which forest and farm products play an important role.

The remarkable feature of the Bhutanese agriculture is not the immense variety of food, vegetables, cash crops and fruits that the country grows but its self-sufficiency in food. Perhaps, the secret lies in the sparse population of the country. Bhutan is a land blessed with plenty of natural resources which had hardly begun to be tapped. Its valleys are fertile. The rainfall is abundant and forests vast and thick. For centuries, trade between Bhutan on one hand and Indian and Tibetan bazaars on the other had brought to the Bhutanese people a measure of economic prosperity. The ancient caravan route saw brisk trade in products like salt, wool, musk, textiles (from west and east) and rice, dyes, silk, cloth, betel nut, tobacco and herbs (from south). Even today, Bhutan's economy is rooted mainly in its natural resources, agriculture and animal husbandry. Bhutan's wealth of cottage industry consists of fine handicrafts of wood and bamboo, ornaments of gold and silver and highly developed weaving skills. New vistas in economy are opening with the building of roads and bridges, factories, hydro-electric power stations and communication network. In the context of Asia and its South Asian neighbours in particular, Bhutan also presents the paradox of under-employment; but it is pushing ahead towards the goal of economic self-sufficiency.

When India was under colonial occupation, Britain had not extended its rule to Bhutan which enjoyed enough internal autonomy to be treated as an independent country. But in 1865, a part of southern Bhutan was annexed by the British, following a series of border disputes. Eventually, a treaty was concluded with the British agreeing to pay Bhutan an annual subsidy. Another treaty was signed in 1910, with the British agreeing not to interfere in Bhutan's internal affairs. In 1949, two years after India became independent, a similar treaty was concluded with the Republic of India.

Till the early 20th century, Bhutan did not have a powerful uniting force as embodied in the king today. For nearly three centuries before that, Bhutan survived under its own style of political system laced with theocracy. The period prior to the 17th century was marked by petty feuds among many local chiefs, each controlling his own territory. Even the monasteries were engaged in a race for superiority.

Many historians agree that the founder of Bhutan was a political refugee from Tibet—a prince and a monk—who came to the tiny landlocked southern neighbour in 1616. Ngawang Namgyal (1594 to 1651) was a monk from the Ralung monastery near Lhasa, representing the Drukpa school. He gave Bhutan a system of secular government based on religious order.

Becoming the temporal and spiritual ruler of Bhutan, he unified much of the country and promulgated his 16 tenets. In the meanwhile, he realised, after repeated attacks from the north, that Bhutan must define itself as an entity different from Tibet and preserve its own religious and cultural identity. Towards this end, he even devised many customs, traditions and ceremonies exclusive to the Bhutanese.

After establishing a dual theocratic system of government and designating himself as the first *Zhabdrung* Rinpoche, he created another system. Under the *Choesi* system, the religious and spiritual matters were entrusted to the *Zhabdrung* while the political, administrative and foreign affairs were under the charge of an elected *Desi*. The *Zhabdrung* became the spiritual leader while the head of the monastic establishment was called the Je Khempo who had the same status as the *Desi* and sometimes even held that office. The first *Desi* was Tenzin Drugyal, one of the monks who had come with Ngawang Namgyal from Ralung.

The instability in Bhutan saw more rounds of Tibetan invasion. The advent of the British rule in India added to the Bhutanese woes as Bhutanese and British interests clashed in certain northern plains in the Bengal region of British India. Bhutan had controlled 18 *duars* (doors) in Cooch Bihar (Bengal). But the British annexed the area from Bhutan.

By March 1865, the British were firmly in control in the area. The Treaty of Sinchula, signed after the conclusion of the war, was to establish peace and friendship between the governments of Bhutan and British India.

Over another 150 years, Bhutan lived under a theocratic political system established by Ngawang Namgyal three hundred years ago. The Zhabdrung Rinpoche acted as the supreme religious and political authority while the *druk desi* (*deb*) was designated the highest civil leader. The Zhabdrung successors were chosen by reincarnation. The central authority delegated powers to *penlops* (governors) and *dzongpons* (district chiefs) to administer different regions. But this system did not guarantee stability, more so when the Zhabdrung successors were minors. There were power clashes between the *penlops* and the *debs*. The Sinchula Treaty only led to gradual weakening of the office of the *deb* and more conflicts within Bhutan.

By the beginning of the 20th century the two strongest political figures to emerge in the country were the *penlops* of Paro and Trongsa who were bitter rivals. At the southern door of Bhutan, the British were busy expanding their empire. For Bhutan the question was whether to make peace with the British or their northern neighbour, Tibet, which was under Chinese influence.

The *Penlop* of Paro was not very enthusiastic about the British. But the *Penlop* of Trongsa, Ugyen Wangchuck and his adviser, Kazi Ugyen Dorji, decided to get closer to the British. Ugyen Wangchuck accompanied a British invasion team, led by Francis Younghusband, to Tibet in 1904. He was able to unite the country and give it a strong central leadership after a gap of 150 years.

On 17 December, 1907, Ugyen Wangchuck was crowned

the first hereditary monarch of Bhutan with the title *Druk Gyalpo* (Dragon King or the Precious Ruler of the Dragon People). He died in 1926 and was succeeded by his 24-year-old son, Jigme Wangchuck, who ruled Bhutan during the time the world witnessed the Second Great War and the Great Depression. While these events had left Bhutan virtually unaffected, the independence of India from the British in August 1947 was probably a more significant development for the Himalayan Kingdom.

King Jigme Wangchuck greatly improved the administration and was able to bring the entire country under his direct control. He saw the newly independent India sign a treaty with Bhutan in 1949, which was, of course, the same treaty that Bhutan had signed with British India earlier in 1910. Under the treaty, Bhutan's status as an independent sovereign state was reaffirmed.

India agreed not to interfere in the internal affairs of Bhutan, and Bhutan accepted India's role in guiding its external relations. Under the terms of the treaty, Bhutan was also able to get back 82 square kilometres of *duars*, including Deothang, that had been taken over by the British.

The death of King Jigme Wangchuck in 1952 brought to the Bhutanese throne his son, King Jigme Dorji Wangchuck, who was educated in India as well as UK. An enlightened man, he did much to modernise Bhutan, constituting the Tshogdu (National Assembly) in 1953 and abolishing serfdom in 1956. He set Bhutan on the path of economic progress, launching the first Five Year Plan in 1961. But he also wanted to ensure that the Bhutanese culture and traditions were preserved in their pristine form.

He brought Bhutan out of its isolation in the world by taking on the membership of many world organisations. But Bhutan's membership of the Universal Postal Union in 1969 can be said to have a special significance for Bhutan. Bhutanese commemorative stamps are

Above: Ugyen Wangchuck, the Penlop of Tongsa had great qualities of leadership. On December 17, 1907 he was proclaimed monarch of Bhutan by the civic and monastic leaders. Thus establishing the hereditary monarchy of Bhutan with the title 'Druk Gyalpo'– precious ruler of the dragon people. After his death in August 1926 he was succeeded by his son (Right) Jigme Wangchuck, who ruled untill his death in 1952.

among the most favourite of the philatelists. In 1971, Bhutan had become a member of the United Nations and in the same year, India and Bhutan established formal diplomatic relationship.

Among the many achievements of King Jigme Dorji Wangchuck can be included abolishing serfdom, drawing up a 12-volume code of law, reorganising land holdings, setting up the country's High Court and raising the Royal Bhutanese army as well as the police force.

King Jigme Dorji Wangchuck died at the young age of 44 in 1972. His son, Jigme Singye Wangchuck, who succeeded him, was only 16 at that time. He was certainly among the youngest monarchs in the world. The young king had the benefit of education in three countries—Bhutan, India and Britain. He has proved to be a very able and well-loved leader of his country. He realised that Bhutan's small population and abundance of natural resources should be used to set the country on the path of economic self-reliance.

Above: King Jigme Dorji Wangchuck was truly the architect of modern Bhutan. His accession to the throne in March 1952, set the country on the path of modernisation. He made Bhutan a member of various world organisations including the United Nations.

A man of modern time, his coronation on 2 June, 1974 at Thimpu was watched by not only his adoring people and dignitaries but a contingent of the international press. This was the first time in the history of Bhutan that foreign press had been allowed entry in the kingdom. In all, 287 foreign guests attended the coronation ceremony. Many hotels had to be built for their stay. It could be said that the young king's coronation was the beginning of the opening of his kingdom to the outside world.

His Majesty Jigme Singye Wangchuck has continued the reforms that his father had introduced in various fields—administration, labour and justice. He has also opened the Bhutanese doors just a little bit more to ensure that the country does not suffer in its development on account of an isolationist policy. He once observed: "By shedding our professional isolationist policy and becoming a member of the United Nations in 1971, we have projected ourselves on the international scene. It is, therefore, important that the world at large should know us a little better."

But he has laid more stress on education, health services, rural development and communications. He upholds the traditional values and culture of Bhutan while being open to fresh ideas. He has also left his imprint on various fields of development. The country is well set on the path to economic progress. As early as 1977, he had told his people:

Sovereignty and self-reliance are two important goals. Whatever we do in the government, it is aimed towards the strengthening and the attainment of these two objectives. But government alone cannot make the country self-reliant. The people have an important role to play. It is important that whatever we do ensures that we retain our sovereignty and helps us become self-reliant.

His Majesty,
King Jigme Singye Wangchuck

Perhaps, his biggest contribution to Bhutan is his concern and dedication to environmental conservation. In Bhutan commercial interests do not outweigh ecological considerations.

The king travels frequently to even the remotest parts of Bhutan. He loves his people and likes open and frank discussions with them, ever ready to answer their queries. In fact, he is available to his people virtually any time. It is his firm belief that his country can march ahead only with the support and participation of all its people. Bhutan enjoys the fruits of democracy under a monarchy.

In 1988, King Jigme Singye Wangchuck married in the traditional Bhutanese style sisters Ashi Dorji Wangmo, Ashi Tshering Pem, Ashi Tshering Yangdon and Ashi Sangay Choedon. The king and his queens have five princes and five princesses. Dasho Jigme Khesar Namgyal Wangchuck is the Crown Prince.

The Bhutanese ruler today is addressed as His Majesty. To address him as His Highness was something of an Indian influence where every ruler of the native states was thus addressed. The Bhutanese king is regarded as The Precious Master and The Supreme Lama. He occupies the 'golden throne', wraps a yellow shawl and wears a 'raven crown' which was originally designed by a lama.

What distinguishes the Bhutan king from other kings and potentates of the world is the serene rural setting of his kingdom. This probably encourages the king to be far more accessible to his people than his high position would allow elsewhere. But even in the absence of a 'modern' urban ambience in his kingdom, he could have surrounded himself in luxury and a life of ostentation. That His Majesty Jigme Singye Wangchuck spurned that kind of lifestyle is a tribute to his qualities. For him, the welfare of his people is of more concern than pomp and show of the court.

Dzongs and Monasteries

After the green of its forests and valleys, and the white snow of its peaks, it is the *dzongs*, monasteries, temples and chortens that dominate the Bhutanese landscape. Wherever one travels these magnificent 'castles' (*dzongs*) in white situated on hilltops or the confluence of rivers stand out as the finest examples of Bhutanese construction and design. Introduced in Bhutan in the 17th century by the first Zhabdrung Ngawang Namgyal, the *dzongs* are the perfect examples of Bhutanese architecture.

The uninitiated may mistake a *dzong* for a big house, but it is easy to distinguish the two because the *dzong* will have a red band on the wall and a banner of victory, the *gyeltshen*, in guilded

Like a fortress, the Dzong at Wangdi Phodrang stands atop a hill overlooking the river Puna Tsang Chhu providing a magnificent view of the valley on both sides.

copper on the roof. In fact, a red band, the *khamar*, is painted in all *dzongs* and religious buildings and it runs just below the roof. One or more circular brass plates or mirrors, representing the sun, are often placed on the *khamar*.

The *dzong* is a building designed to serve three functions. It is a fortress, a monastery and the administrative-cum-judicial centre of the region in which it is situated. The *dzong* is unique in style, yet a general layout pattern is followed. An astonishing thing about the *dzongs* is that they are constructed without the aid of a design or drawing. No nails are used in the construction of these massive buildings. It all comes out of a concept matured perfectly over three centuries in the mind of the builder.

Repeated needs to build and rebuild them must have

Below:
Paro Dzong by the side of
Paro Chhu

Following double spread:
A majestic view of the
Thimpu Dzong

Double spread pages 46-47:
Inner courtyard of the
Thimpu Dzong

Double spread pages 48-49:
Inner courtyard of the
Paro Dzong is a classic
example of Bhutanese art
and architecture.

further consolidated the mental design of *dzongs*. The reason was simple. Despite the use of pounded mud, a lot of wood is used in the superstructure of *dzongs* as a result of which they have been frequently damaged or destroyed by fire. There are not many *dzongs* which have not required repair or reconstruction. But many of the fires that harmed them were caused by the butter lamps which were overturned, setting wall hangings or paintings on fire. In recent years, however, iron sheets have supplanted the shingles as roofing material of the *dzongs*.

The first seat of power in Bhutan was located in a *dzong*, which explains why they served as fortresses and watch-towers for defence. They were also built to assimilate with the surrounding terrain. A *dzong* has an inward sloping wall with one

Memorial Chorten at Thimpu

massive door leading to a small passage. Two right-angle turns later is reached the main courtyard. It is a quadrilateral of buildings that enclose one or more courtyards. The religious and civil quarters are divided by a central tower, the *utse*. A *dzong* is decorated by a complex wood carving and paintings. The main courtyard of the *dzong* is the *dochey* which is paved with large flagstones. Overlooking the paved courtyard are several rooms and galleries which serve as living quarters and classrooms for the monks. The multi-purpose Bhutanese *dzongs* have acquired a distinctive character of their own over the centuries.

Chortens are the most common architectural feature of the countryside in Bhutan. *Chortens* are also Buddhist monuments and are receptacles of worship offerings. Their origin can be traced

Chorten at Kurizampa

to the stupas of ancient India. A *chorten* is built as votive monument in the memory of the Buddha or his many admirable deeds. It is also a monument to the memory of important religious figures and monks who had contributed to the spread of Buddhism. Though there are variations in the architecture of the *chorten*, the ones found in Bhutan generally resemble a house. Symbolically, the *chorten*, which is a smaller shrine than a *dzong*, consists of five parts, representing the five elements of the cosmos—earth, water, fire, air and ether.

It is believed that after the cremation of the body of Lord Buddha the relics were divided into eight groups for as many claimants. Each of the eight claimants erected a monument or *stupa* which were originally simple in design but, with the passage of time, acquired complex tones. Some are simple square structures

A row of chortens by the road side between Khaling and Kanglung

with only the most rudimentary motifs. Others are multi-layered structures, pyramidal in shape and lavishly decorated.

Initially, a *chorten* housed relics of the Buddha or other Buddhist saints; but as time progressed, these monuments acquired great significance and symbolism, and came to be seen as great acts of piety for those who built them or paid for their construction.

There are *chortens* that are close to *dzongs* while many others are in remote forests or mountain passes, far removed from human habitation. The most common of the eight forms of *chortens* seen in Bhutan is called the *khangtseg*, or the house *chorten*. It is a simple building, square in shape with an ornamental roof and containing the sacred relics.

All *chortens* are sacred and exude a feeling of peace and serenity. The more sacred among them bring unparalleled spiritual benefits. Circumambulating the most sacred ones, such as the ones at Jampa and Paro, is equal to circumambulating and prostrating before 100,000 other lesser *chortens*. And circumambulating is considered the most pious and effective means of purifying oneself.

Among the other religious buildings that abound in Bhutan are *lhakhangs* or temples and, of course, monasteries. For a country of its size and population, Bhutan has a very large number of religious buildings. All of them were built for different purposes to suit the wishes of their builders or sponsors. A *lhakhang* can be part of a *dzong* or independent of it. Outside a *lhakhang* stand a series of prayer wheels which are rotated by pilgrims as they go round the sacred place.

The monasteries were built in remote and isolated places to provide peace and solitude for the monks. Many were built on top of rocks or distant hills. But several monasteries were built in sacred caves which were at one time places of meditation.

The monasteries, or the *goembas*, are self-contained. They may be different but all of them share certain common features. The living quarters are segregated from the prayer area, which is in the centre of the courtyard and also serves as the dancing area for the monks during the many festivals.

With such a plethora and variety of religious buildings, it is natural that Bhutanese assign an important place to monastic life. Time has, however, made one difference. It is no longer possible to expect every family to send at least one of its sons to a monastery. As a result, monks do not dominate the male population in Bhutan, though they continue to constitute a large percentage of it. Monks also continue to play an important part in the everyday life of Bhutanese.

The future monks begin their life in the monasteries at an early age, usually between five and six years, though a boy considered an incarnation may begin at the age of three. Their tutors are elderly and educated monks.

Life in the monasteries is disciplined in accordance with

The picturesque monastery at Rang Jung

religious canons. The pupils learn to read and write, and participate in various ceremonies. They also learn by heart the rich and extensive literature that includes texts of the *Kanjur* (collection of Buddha's words) and the *Tenjur* (collection of commentaries on the *Kanjur*) as well as complete works of well-known religious teachers and treatises on subjects like philosophy, medicine and astrology. The young pupils emerge from their schools as monks well-versed in elaborate rites and rituals which are accompanied by many musical instruments like cymbals and drums.

The altar at religious places in Bhutan are very well decorated, complete with butter lamps, colourful objects and cakes. Monks of the Drukpa monasteries have to take a vow of celibacy.

A young lama boy on an errand at Mongar Dzong

But certain monks of the Nyingmapa order need not take this vow and may marry.

The monks visit families to perform rituals and also the rites at the time of birth, wedding or death in a family. The rich Bhutanese have one or more monks stay as their guests for varying length of time. The house with a monk guest or guests is considered well-protected and enjoys some spiritual merit.

Besides the ordained monks, Bhutan has another category, called the *gomchen*, who generally live in the eastern part of the country. They are peasants who lead family life but are given the responsibility of performing rituals in temples and private homes on certain occasions.

Below:
Monasteries in Bhutan have a huge collection of Buddhist manuscripts

Right:
A young lama lost in thoughts at the Paro Dzong

Festivals and Dances

Festivals and dances go hand in hand in Bhutan. If the festivals are almost always religious in nature, the dances, which can be performed by both monks and laymen, are morally instructive. It is said of Bhutanese dances that they represent the most faithful form of ancient Himalayan dances.

The most famous religious festival is called *Tshechu*. which is celebrated in all the *dzongs* and many temples to commemorate different events in the life of Guru Rinpoche. Attending the Tshechu dance, being a religious festival, is said to bestow merit. Deities are invoked during the dance. Their powers are such that misfortunes can be eliminated, luck increased and wishes realised. Everyone comes out in his or her best clothes. The festival is also a joyous social gathering and an occasion for exchange of news.

The duration of the Tshechu festival, its dates and its programme vary from place to place. The programmes are not rigid: dances can be added or omitted. Though most dances are performed all over Bhutan, certain dances are specific to a place.

Dances performed on secular occasions like the coronation of the king or the celebration of the national day also have a touch of religion. First of all the most auspicious day is chosen for the event. Monks are at hand to bless the day.

Bhutanese dances are energetic and graceful. Wearing colourful clothes and robes, the dancers bend and leap high in the air, their robes flowing and swirling and their hands, with or without a sword, moving in various gestures. Dances are performed to the accompaniment of a host of musical instruments like trumpets, drums, cymbals, pipes and gongs as stories from

Below and Left:
A dance performance in the courtyard of Paro Dzong during the annual festival

Following double spread:
A huge tankha on display at Paro Dzong during the annual festival. The precious tankha is brought out at night and is rolled back before the first rays of sunlight fall on it.

Double spread pages 62-63:
Dances during the Mongar festival

Below and left:
Dances during the
Mongar festival

65

the Bhutanese history and mythology are presented before appreciative audiences. A common theme is demons being vanquished by the heroes and believers driving out the non-believers.

During many *Tshechus*, a large *thangka* (religious painting) is unfurled before sunrise from the building overlooking the dance area. The large painting, called *thongdrol*, washes away the sins of those who look at it. Often, a small fair is set up outside the *dzong* where the *Tshechu* festival is held.

One of the most famous dances is called the Black Hat which is about a Tibetan king, Langdarma, who ruled between AD 803 and 842. He was a follower of the Bon faith and had persecuted and killed many Buddhist monks. A monk disguised himself as a priest of the Bon faith and gained entry into the king's court. At

Below:
Zhana Chhham (Black Hat dance). The dance is performed to subdue the enemies of the doctrine and pacify evil spirits.

Right:
Due Nagpo (Black demon) during the Raksha Mangcham

the opportune time he pulled out an arrow he had hidden in his sleeve to slay the tyrannical king.

Tshechu dances are varied and elaborate, performed over a number of days. In one day the range of dances can begin with the story of how Guru Rinpoche subdued the God of the Wind, going on to the visual representation of the paradise of Guru Rinpoche, as seen by Pema Lingpa, and move to the story of how the demons working against religion were subdued. The next item could depict the story of a hunter who was converted to Buddhism by a saint. The first day may end with a cheerful dance to celebrate the beginning of the Drukpa lineage in Bhutan.

Below:
Khimdag Palkye, a virtuous man, on the day of Judgement, the Raksha Mangcham.

Many of the dances are the composition of Zhabdrung Ngawang Namgyal and Pema Lingpa. The performers represent the wrathful and the compassionate aspects of deities, heroes,

demons and animals. The dancers bring blessings upon the onlookers, who are instructed on Buddhism and protected from misfortune. The dancers also exorcise the evil influences.

There are many lay dances too. Every Bhutanese knows their basic steps and the songs that go with them. After 1959, when Tibetan refugees arrived in Bhutan, Tibetan dances, particularly the Yak dance, have also become popular.

In the south of the country with its large population of people of Nepalese origin, the slow and graceful Nepalese dances are very popular.

On important occasions, one can see all types of dances performed in one place. Dancing is in the Bhutanese blood, they cannot be separated from their dances.

Below:
A group song and dance at the Paro festival.

Religion and Art

Religion

Religion has an all-pervasive influence in Bhutan and the life of its people. The pull of religion affects even the Bhutanese art—so also its dance, drama and music. Buddhism plays a key role in the cultural, ethical and social development of the country.

Bhutan is the only country in the world that retains the tantric (Vajrayana) form of Mahayana Buddhism, called Drukpa Kagyu, as its official religion. It is somewhat similar to the form of Buddhism practised in Tibet. The Vajrayana Buddhism was born out of Mahayana traditions in India. Bhutan's Drukpa Kagyu lineage was established by Tsangpa Jarey Yeshey Dorji at Ralung monastery in Tibet. In the first half of the 13th century, a lama (monk) from the Drukpa monastery at Ralung, Phajo Drukgom Zhigpo, came to Bhutan and established the Drukpa school. Many in Bhutan today trace their ancestry to this monk.

In 1616, a highly respected Drukpa Lama, Zhabdrung Ngawang Namgyal, came to Bhutan after the Ralung monastery had been closed. He established the Drukpa sect as the official state religion. Since then it has remained so, though the Nyingma lineage, the old 'Red Hat' school, also has a significant following.

Above:
An Image of Buddha at the Mongar Dzong

Right:
Jamphala, God of wealth.

Far right:
Huge prayer wheels at the Thimpu Chorten

70

The history of modern Bhutan dates from the arrival of this great 17th century monk. Ngawang Namgyal ruled for 35 years during which he consolidated the authority of the Drukpa sect throughout most of Bhutan. He also set up an administrative system which was replaced only at the beginning of the last century when Bhutan adopted the system of hereditary monarchy.

As witness to the people's faith in religion stand the innumerable religious monuments in every corner of the tiny kingdom. Wherever one goes one can find prayer wheels turning and religious flags waving in the breeze, sending the message of the Buddha from populated valleys, mountain slopes, bridges and high passes to desolate and remote mountains. The lonely alpine passes have the sacred mantra, *Om Mani Padme Hun*, carved on stones and hillsides.

Preceding pages

Double spread pages 72-73:
Colourful prayer flags are a
common sight in Bhutan.

pages 74-75:
At the Mongar Dzong, a lama poses
in front of Sithpai Khorlo, wheel of
existence showing the six realms:
Gods, demigods,
human beings, animals, hungry
ghosts and the hell.

Below:
Tsepame Yab Yum, a fresco at the
Mongar Dzong.

Every home has a shrine room, *choesham*, where the family prays at the altar. The altar has usually statues of the three great lamas—Sakyamuni, Guru Rinpoche and Zhabdrung Rinpoche. Seven bowls filled with water are placed at the altar as offerings to deities.

The Bhutanese landscape is full of *chortens*, housing sacred relics. The *chortens* ward off evil spirits and protect travellers as well as residents from danger. Symbolically, the *chortens* represent the mind of the Buddha. Life in every village and town revolves round monasteries and temples.

An interesting fact about Bhutan is that the holy shrines in the country were built by voluntary labour. The Bhutanese believe that participating in the building of shrines and holy places is an important act of faith.

Though it may not be entirely true today, every Bhutanese family has been traditionally sending one son to attend monastic schools located in *dzongs*.

Below:
An old chorten stands guard at the enterance of Mongar

77

Each district has its annual festivals, Tshechu and Dromchoes, which are considered spiritual occasions dedicated to guru Rinpoche or other deities. The temples in the area are decorated with treasured *thangkas*, which are intricately painted scrolls depicting scenes from Buddhist mythology. Dancers and musicians bring alive stories from the past. The festivities last several days and are accompanied by archery competition and picnics.

Every district has a *dzong* which is a defensive and impregnable fortress. It is the centre of both religious and secular activities. It also houses the area's monk body.

The head of Bhutan's body of monks, the Je Khenpo, is a highly respected figure. He commands almost the same respect as the monarch. The monks are also greatly respected in Bhutan. They play an important part in community life. The monks are

Below:
Prayer flags fluttering over Kuri Chu river

Right:
The head of Bhutan's monk body– Je Khenpo—blessing the audience at the Mongar festival

Above:
An old picture of Taksang monastery, popularly known as 'The Tiger's Nest', perched on a 3,000 feet high cliff, as it stood before it was destroyed in a fire in 1997.

Right:
The new structure of Taksang monastery now under construction

represented on all important occasions. They hold seats in the National Assembly and the Royal Advisory Council.

After the Buddha, the most revered figure in Bhutan is Padmasambhava who had brought Buddhism to the country. While still a child, he had acquired profound knowledge and mystic powers from some famous teachers at India's Nalanda University.

Padmasambhava introduced the Nyingmapa School of Buddhism to Tibet. He went to Bumthang, Bhutan on an invitation from Sindhu Raja who was suffering from a severe ailment. Legend has it that he came to Bhutan on the back of a tigress. The Tiger Nest in the Paro Valley perpetuates that legend. After his arrival in Bumthang, Padmasambhava held the first festival of ritual dances, representing the triumph of good over evil. Sindhu Raja was cured and converted to Buddhism.

A number of temples and monasteries are associated with Padmasambhava. One of them is at a 3,000-feet cliff, Taktsang, where the demons standing in the wave of spreading Buddhism were vanquished. It attracts pilgrims from all over Bhutan.

In Bumthang, the Kurje temple is built at a site where Padmasambhava had meditated and left his fingerprints and body prints etched on a solid rock. A cypress tree at the site, which still stands, grew out of his wooden staff.

Padmasambhava's teachings are known as *termas* (the term is also used for sacred objects). Traditionally, they were hidden underground or in caves to be 'discovered' by the chosen ones at appropriate times in the future. The reason for their being so hidden was the people being not ready to receive the teachings. Bhutan came to be known as the Land of Hidden Treasures because many of these *termas* were hidden here.

Art

One distinct characteristic of the Bhutanese art is that it is anonymous. The artist almost never writes his name on his work. Art in Bhutan is not used for self-expression, nor is it taken up for art's sake. Like early Indian art, it is devoted mainly to the preservation of deities. The Bhutanese believe that making or painting a deity is a pious act that leads to salvation.

It is taken up on behalf of a patron (*jinda*) whose name may appear in the work so that his contribution to the pious act is remembered.

The Bhutanese do not give much importance to self-expression in art but they regard contemplation and visualisation of colours as an integral part of meditation. It takes the believer closer to the goal of enlightenment. Age-old credos dictate the form of patterns of Bhutanese art. There is a strong feeling of beauty, line and colour in the Bhutanese works of art—painting, sculpture, carvings and so on. Bhutanese art concentrates on iconographical accuracy and verity of form. The depiction of divine figures is almost a part of meditation and devotion.

A notable feature of Bhutanese art is that it enjoys the patronage and support of all sections of the society, from the royal family and nobility to the monks and the common people who depend on the artisans to supply them the wide variety of wooden and metal objects they need in their houses.

It may be noted that the late King Jigme Dorji Wangchuck provided a big impetus to the cultural life of the country. He was very keen that the traditional art of Bhutan be preserved. But that required an adequate patronage. He, therefore, made arrangements to train new artists under the guidance of the chief painting master of the state monastery in Tashichho Dzong. After their training, these artists were employed by the government to paint murals and *thangkas* and to decorate government buildings all over the country.

The Bhutanese tradition defines 13 different forms of arts (*zorig chusum*) that are practised in the country. Even activities like carpentry and weaving are part of Bhutan's heritage of *zorig chusum* and the country's artistic traditions.

The painting tradition is called *lhazo* and includes *thangkas*, the religious scroll paintings, wall paintings and decorative paintings.

Carpentry is called *shingzo* or wood art, which serves the task of construction of *dzongs*, monasteries, houses and household goods.

Carving, or *parzo*, on wood, slate or stone is an important art. Most religious texts are printed from wooden blocks on which the monks have carved a mirror image of the text.

Sculpture or *jinzo* (mud work) includes clay statues, ritual objects like drum stands, *torma* (ritual cakes) and masks. Construction work, using mortar, plaster and rammed earth are also included in it.

Painting a Thangka is a very slow and demanding process that requires great skills.

There are two types of casting, or *lugzo*, using sand and lost wax. *Lugzo* craftsmen produce statues, bells, ritual instruments, jewellery and kitchen equipments.

Cane and bamboo works, or *tshazo*, are part of one craft which is used in making bows and arrows, hats, mats, baskets for various uses, including storing grain and bamboo thatch.

The blacksmith, or *chazo*, makes many iron goods, such as swords, knives, chisels, axes, spades, shovels, darts, helmets, chains and plough blades.

A large number of household goods are made by the goldsmiths and silversmiths, or *zero ngulzo*. The things they make include jewellery, ritual objects, brooches, chains, rings, trumpets, cymbals and amulets.

The entire process, starting from preparation of yarn to dyeing and the final weaving is called *thagzo*.

Embroidery, called *tshemzo*, is of two categories. The traditional embroidery, *tshendrup*, includes boot making; while the one involving applique work, called *lhendrup*, requires sewing of pieces of cloth into a picture shape.

Cutting and stacking stone walls is the art of masonry, or *dozo*, which is specifically applied to the construction of huge outer stone walls of *dzongs*, monasteries and other buildings.

Craftsmen of leather works, or *lozo*, make items like *gayu*, the leather bags for carrying grain, and *shadha*, leather ropes and belts for swords.

The paper work art is called *dezo*. The traditional paper is made from the daphne (De) plant.

Above:
Wood carving is an old tradition in Bhutan.

Facing page:
'The cosmic mandala' is almost like a graph of the atomic movement. This powerful fresco at the enterance of Paro Dzong in western Bhutan, is not a meditation mandala but perhaps a graphic interpretation to illustrate the origin of the universe.

"A Bhutanese is nothing if not outgoing." Any occasion is good enough for a celebration with dancing, singing, sporting events and much merry-making. Festivities are a perennial feature of Bhutanese life. They carry their irrepressible nature to their daily grind in the fields and construction sites. Occasions for celebrations are many: birth, wedding, even death and illness, voyage, promotion, construction, annual blessings of the household or any religious ceremony.

A famous 18th century visitor summed up the Bhutanese well:

> The simplicity of their manners, their slight intercourse with strangers, and a strong sense of religion, preserve the Bhutanese from many vices to which more polished nations are addicted. They are strangers to falsehood and ingratitude.

Left:
Garlands of dried cheese outside shops make a fascinating display

Below:
Bhutanese women carry their young ones on back and go about their routine work in a very relaxed manner.

93

Theft and every other species of dishonesty to which the lust of money gives birth are little known.

Indeed, the simplicity of the Bhutanese manners is uncommon; and so is their solid common sense and concern for others. Arrogance is alien to their nature as is any complex. The Bhutanese are very proud of their traditions and customs, their political system and their religion, all of which give them a distinct identity of their own. The Bhutanese spirit of tolerance must be a direct result of their adherence to Buddhist codes; but they also observe a strict code of etiquette that reflects a complex hierarchical system. The superiors have to be shown special respect; but when people of same rank get together they let their hair down.

Below:
Bhutan's younger generation and the government both are keen on education.

As an act of courtesy and hospitality, the Bhutanese offer a gift of the *doma*, an areca nut coated in lime and wrapped in a betel leaf.

Bhutanese live in large joint families where both male and female members work. Men and women enjoy equal rights; but the females bring additional income through their supplementary activities like weaving and shopkeeping.

Divorce and remarriages are also frequent, though it can often lead to complications. A divorce case can be settled in a court or through mutual consent in the presence of elders and honoured persons.

Yet, the Bhutanese society is strongly egalitarian in nature. There is no rigid class system. Social and educational opportunities are equal for all. The family system is patriarchal. The family property is divided equally between sons and daughters though disputes over inheritance also arise.

Of the three main ethnic groups in Bhutan, the Sharchops, who are of Indo-Mongoloid origin, are the earliest inhabitants, living largely in eastern Bhutan.

The descendants of the Tibetan immigrants from the ninth century onwards settled largely in the western part of the country. They are known as the Ngalops. The people of Nepalese origin, now refered as *Lhotsampas,* began to arrive in the southern part of Bhutan around the end of the 19th century.

Dzongkha, a dialect akin to Tibetan, is Bhutan's official language, written in the Ucan script. Over the years Dzongkha has acquired local tones based on peculiarities of pronunciation. About a dozen different dialects, not necessarily derived from Dzongkha, are spoken in the eastern part of the kingdom. Often, it is difficult for the speaker of one of these dialects to understand the speaker of another dialect.

English was introduced in the 1960s as a medium of instruction in secular schools. But the classical form of Dzongkha, called Cheokay, is used in traditional monastic schools.

Eastern Bhutan

The districts of Trashigang and Mongar constitute the main parts of Eastern Bhutan together with a southern portion that goes up to Samdrup Jongkhar. Eastern Bhutan is comparatively densely populated and may be considered the hinterland of the land-locked kingdom. It is a region of deep valleys where fields and human habitats appear glued to the base of mountain slopes. Maize is the main crop here but rice and wheat is also grown. Among its cattle wealth, the most famous is *mithun*, a native bull with prominent horns. Houses generally conform to the Bhutanese style but there are many bamboo matting houses that are raised on stilts.

In the extreme east of the country are the valleys of Sakteng and Merak where live semi-nomadic herdsmen, identified easily

The neat little market of Trashigang

with their yak-hair hats, who are classified as a separate ethnic group. The Sharchops of East Bhutan speak a language known as Tshangla which is very different from the official language.

The people, who are of Mongoloid origin, are friendly, informal but deeply religious. There are places where one can see people chatting—near their homes, shops or even in the middle of the road.

Eastern Bhutan is separated from the rest of the country by deep gorges and steep mountains through which a number of rivers meander their way towards India. The drive through many parts of the region can be a feast for the eye through roads and passes by the side of the hills and steep climbs and descends. What makes the drive more spectacular is the sight of forests of rhododendrons of many colours amidst valleys and ridges.

Below:
Merak people from the extreme east of Bhutan are easily recognised by their distinctly different features and typical headgear made of yak hair.

Following double spread:
Women of eastern Bhutan weaving outdoors on their makeshift looms on a foggy day

97

Most of the villages in the region are situated on mountain slopes which are often deforested. In the rest of the country, the villages are situated in the open valleys. At lower altitudes, lesser forestcover is quite apparent.

Yak is a common animal that can be seen dominating the high altitude pasture land in the springtime. During the harsh winter months, many from the region prefer to go the western part of Bhutan, carrying with them their prized butter and wooden vessels for trading.

Trashigang, the largest district, is also in eastern Bhutan. It is home to about 150,000 people and, after Thimpu, the biggest urban centre in the mountains. It is also the heart of eastern Bhutan. Situated at the foot of a wooded but a steep valley on the banks of Damgenchu river, it is rich in tropical crops and fruits. The climate

The only degree college of the country is located in the picturesque town of Kanglung in eastern Bhutan

is generally pleasant though the more pleasant aspect is the sight of the colourful bougainvillea creepers. The town is connected to Samdrup Jongkhar town near the Indian border by a metalled road. In old days, Trashigang was famous for its trade links with Tibet. Local traders would take rice, maize, chillies, indigenous paints and silk to return with salt, wool and tea from Tibet.

A handloom industry also thrives in Trashigang. Trashigang's Endi silk is something special as it is spun from cocoons bred on caster plants unlike the usual silk cocoons that are bred on mulberry.

There are several *goembas* in the district. The 17th century Trashigang Dzong at the top of a spur overlooks the confluence of two rivers and commands an impressive view of the countryside. It looks like an impregnable fort surrounded by rivers and ravines on three sides and a mountain at the back. It was from this *dzong* that Eastern Bhutan was governed from late 17 to the 20th century. The *dzong*, like so many other *dzongs* in the country, was destroyed in a fire and rebuilt.

Mongar, like many towns in east Bhutan, rests on the side of a mountian amidst maize fields and eucalyptus trees. If East Bhutan towns are not built in a valley it is because the valleys of the region are generally nothing more than river beds. The mountains in East Bhutan can rise suddenly from the rivers.

The town was built almost anew in 1997 when a large part of the bazaar was rebuilt. The *dzong* was also renovated in 1990

Above:
Women of eastern Bhutan are famous for their skill of weaving very intricate patterns.

Following double spread:
A panoramic view of the serpentine road passing through a lush green valley, west of Mongar

101

At the foothills of the tall snow-clad mountains of the north lies central Bhutan where valleys are situated at heights between 1,800 and 2,750 metres. Valleys like Punakha and Wangdiphodrang are comparatively at lower heights, but Thimpu and other valleys are near 2,440 metres high. Dark forests of oak, birch, maple, magnolia and laurel abound in the temperate zone. At heights of over 2,400 metres, yew and weeping cypress are found, and at still higher heights can be seen the Himalayan fir. Between 2,250 and 2,850 metres a variety of high altitude oak is found, and at higher elevations are forests of birch. The valleys are swept by strong winds. The average annual rainfall is 1,000 mm. The winters here are extremely cold, the temperature touching minus 10 degree C.

The variety of vegetation in the temperate zone is fascinating: rhododendrons, poplar, willow, walnut, ash, aspen and magnolia. The conifers found include blue pine, hemlock, larch and fir. Autumn sees the mauve pink flowers of the Himalayan wild cherry blooming at heights between 1,200 metres and 3,000 metres.

In the months of March, April and May, the landscape is dominated by the rhododendron. Once the national flower of Bhutan, rhododendron is popularly known here as *Etho Metho*.

Bhutan's national flower now is the blue poppy, which can be blue or purple with a white filament. The plant grows to be nearly one metre tall on rocky mountain terrain at an altitude of 4,000 metres or above. It flowers between late May and July. Its seed yields oil. It has a life of several years though, as a monocarpic plant, it blooms only once. It can be found at high passes almost all across the country.

Interestingly, the existence of blue poppy was not confirmed till almost the middle of the 20th century. For a very long time it remained a myth—like the yeti. But in 1933 a British botanist, George Sherriff, found the plant in the remote Sakteng region in

Above:
In the spring months rhododendron dominate the mountain landscape

Right:
Iris is a very common wild flower in Bhutan

eastern Bhutan. But still not many Bhutanese have seen it. For them there is still an element of mystery about the blue poppy.

In the sub-alpine and alpine zones are low shrubs, rhododendrons, Himalayan grass and flowering herbs at about 5,500 metres. At heights of 4,000 metres are found a dwarf form of junipers with distinctive foliage, sharp needles and red-brown bark. They have a fleshy fruit as well. Other species found are lichens, mosses and alpine flowers that include tiny rhododendrons, nivale, edelweiss and primula.

At the end of winter when snow starts to melt and through the summer months, the grazing lands are covered by a multitude of wild flowers. In the monsoon months of July, August and September the varieties seen include anemones, forget-me-nots, dwarf irisis, dwarf rhododendrons, primulas, delphiniums and ranunculus.

Northern Bhutan is part of the majestic Himalayas which are always covered in snow. The high rugged peaks tower over 7,000 metres. The 7,300 metre high Jhomolhari peak at the north-west border is held sacred by the Bhutanese. It was successfully climbed by an Indo-Bhutanese team in April 1970.

Bhutan's vegetation is as rich as it is varied. But the kind of vegetation found in an area depends on the elevation and the amount of rainfall received. In the tropical region, the vegetation is broad-leaved. Tall savannah grass is also found. The temperate vegetation consists of both broad-leaved trees and conifers.

The alpine region offers an amazing spectacle of multi-coloured rhododendrons along with many other flowering plants. There are extensive pasture grounds.

South Bhutan is known for its abundant and rich crops of citrus fruits, particularly orange and lemon, as also jack-fruit, pineapple and banana. The southern foothills of up to 1,070 metres are good for cultivating pineapple, litchi, mango, orange, guava, areca nut and even cardamom.

Apple, plum, peach, pear and walnut grow in central Bhutan. The valleys of Paro, Thimpu, Ha, Bumthang and Gasa, situated at heights varying from 1,830 metres to 3,050 metres, are ideal for apple, walnut, peach, plum, apricot and almond.

The Bhutanese landscape is dotted with valleys which are important in the economic life of the country. The Ha valley in the extreme west grows wheat, barley, millet and potatoes. Until China took total control of Tibet, the Ha valley was a busy trading centre with goods piled on long caravans of horses and mules.

Punakha valley and dzong

One of the most beautiful and fertile valleys of Bhutan, the Paro valley, lies to the east of the Ha valley. The Pachu river passes through it. At the centre of the valley stands the Rinpung *Dzong* which housed the National Assembly before it moved to the new *dzong* at Thimpu.

Moving east of Paro one will see the valleys of Wang district which has its headquarters at Thimpu, the capital of Bhutan. In the extreme north-west of the district and close to the border with Tibet is the Lingshi *Dzong* which offers a captivating view of the perennial snow peaks.

The Punakha valley lies north-east of Thimpu. South of Punakha lies the wide valley of Sha district. The valley with its vast green pastures has a rich cattle wealth.

To the east of Sha district is the Mangde valley with its

Below:
Trongsa Dzong, the seat of Trongsa Penlops who governed the eastern region.

Following double spread:
The view of Gangchentag Peak from Lingshi.

Trongsa Dzong on the banks of the Mangdechu river. It was from Trongsa that the whole of eastern Bhutan was controlled for centuries. And it was the Governor of Trongsa, Sir Ugyen Wangchuck, who was elected the first hereditary king of Bhutan in 1907.

The Bumthang valley is next to Trongsa with its *dzong* at Jakar. The broad and impressive valley is situated at a height of 2,750 metres. For the Bhutanese, this valley has a special place in their hearts because it was at Kurje in Bumthang that Guru Padmasambhava performed his miraculous feats. It was also here that Pema Lingapa, accepted as an incarnation of Guru Padmasambhava, discovered hidden spiritual treasures from the bottom of Mebar lake.

East of Bumthang, the valley of Kurtoe is known for its

Below:
Lingshi Dzong, close to the
northern border

116

woven fabrics of intricate designs which are much fancied by the rich. An ancestor of the present king belonged to this district.

Next to Kurtoe is Trashigang, Bhutan's largest district. At one time it was also a centre for barter trade with Tibet, exchanging rice, maize, chillies, silk and indigenous paints for salt, wool and tea. The Trashigang district, which boasts a handloom industry, is well-known for its Endi silk spun from cocoons bred on caster plants (instead of the traditional mulberry).

Another area which makes handloom products is the Kheng district with its headquarters at Zhemgang; but it is perhaps better known for its artistic bamboo and metal work.

South of Thimpu and north of Tsirang is the small district of Dagana which is known for its thick hand-made paper manufactured from the pulp of the *daphne* tree.

Below:
Jakar Dzong in Bumthang.

Following double spread:
A section of the Trongsa Dzong.

Tsirang and Samtse are two districts in the southern foothills. Phuentsholing, the gateway to western Bhutan, is in Chukha district. Bhutan's major hydroelectric projects and industries are also located in this area. The Tsirang valley is thickly populated, and is largely inhabited by *Lhotsampas*. Orange grows in abundance in the area and finds market not only in Bhutan but also in neighbouring India and Bangladesh.

Being a mountainous country, Bhutan has a number of rivers, all except two of which rise from the snowy areas in the north and flowing south all the way to India where they merge in the mighty Brahmaputra river.

Phuentsholing, the gateway to Bhutan is a busy little town with lot of industrial and trade activity

The Bhutanese believe that that rivers are the abode of various spirits which have to be placated on all occasions. But the rivers are not considered sacred as they are in India. The rivers,

which are rich in fish and lend colour to the landscape, have tremendous electricity generation potential which can make Bhutan a very 'powerful' country.

Wild Life

Bhutan has a rich fauna of 165 species of mammals. Its wild life includes tiger, leopard, wild buffalo, bison and many species of deer. Wild tuskers are also found in the country.

Takin is Bhutan's national animal. A full grown takin is more than one metre tall and can weigh as much as 1,000 kg. The golden yellow or brown coloured animal looks like a cross

between a gnu and a musk deer with short thick legs and a heavy body. It is generally found in the north-west and the far north-east of the country. The takin is part of Bhutan's history and mythology. It is believed that the 15th century saint, Drukpa Kunley, the divine madman, was once asked by a large gathering of devotees to perform a miracle. He demanded a cow and a goat for lunch before he agreed to do what the assembly wanted. He devoured the animals with relish, leaving only their bones. He then took the goat's head and stuck it into the bones of the cow. Snapping his fingers, he commanded the beast to rise and graze in the mountain. Lo and behold, the strange looking animal that came to be known as *dong gyem tsey* sprang on its feet and ran off to the meadows!

The golden langur is an exclusive species of Bhutan which is not found anywhere else. The existence of this small primate of distinct golden coat was not even known until about a 100 years ago. There are in all three species of monkeys in Bhutan. The rhesus monkey are earth coloured with short tails and travel on the ground. They live in the *duars* close to the Indian border and up to a height of 2,400 metres. The black-faced langur has grey fur and long tails. It lives at altitudes of up to 3,600 metres.

Left: A very rare picture of tiger phographed at an altitude of 3,000 metres in Thrumshingla park.

*Below:
Golden Langur is an exclusive species of Bhutan*

121

A rare species of the blue bear, called *dremo*, belonging to north Bhutan is apparently not very popular among the local population. A common belief is that sighting this bear brings bad luck.

Another fascinating species of the bear is called the *churra*, a pale-yellow creature with thick long-matted hair which reach down to the feet of the animal. It is found at an altitude of over 3,660 metres.

Other animals found in Bhutan include the elephant, snow leopard, tiger and other species of cats, rhino, panda, wild dogs, goat, antelope, wolf, yak, water buffalo, gaur and wild pig.

Birds

Thanks to Bhutan's biodiversity and its ecological environment, nearly 700 species of birds can be sighted in Bhutan, though their variety is seasonal and can change between short distances. A large species of birds are native to Bhutan, but the country also receives migratory birds. There is also a migration of birds within the country, from one climatic zone to another. Some stay in transit for short duration while in flight from Tibet to India.

Among the rare and endangered species seen in Bhutan mention may be made of the migratory black-necked crane which the Bhutanese call *thrung thrung*. Arriving from Tibet in autumn, it is a bird round which revolve many myths and legends. The bird also inspires many songs and dances. It chooses its winter home in the high mountain valleys of Bhutan. It is believed that there are less than 6,000 birds of this species in the world—in Tibet, Ladakh (India) and Bhutan.

There are many other high altitude birds—like the lammergeier, the Himalayan griffon, the isibill and raven, the national bird of Bhutan.

Other species include the blue whistling thrush, yellow billed blue magpies, the wallcreeper, white capper water redstarts, plumbeous water redstarts, spotted nutcrackers and red billed choughs.

A migratory bird like Pallas' fish eagle comes with a large

company of ospreys, ducks and waders. The migratory birds travel from higher altitudes to lower altitudes to escape the harshness of winter. Among such birds can be mentioned rosefinches, grossbeaks, snow pigeons and varieties of pheasants. Generally speaking, egrets, coromants, parakeets, woodpeckers and hornbills are found at the foothills. The colourful sunbirds, titts, flycatchers and the Himalayan pheasants with their attractive feathers live at higher altitudes.

There are many species which are totally protected. The raven is one of them. Other birds include black-necked crane, monal pheasant, peacock pheasant and rufous-necked hornbill.

National Parks

For a country of its size and resources, Bhutan has a good number of wildlife sanctuaries and national parks. About a quarter of the country is protected area which includes human habitation. People living in these areas are allowed to graze animals, do farming and cut firewood.

A unique sanctuary in the world is the Sakteng Wildlife Sanctuary which is the only reserve in the world for the yeti, called *migoi* in Bhutan. The Bhutanese believe their yeti has its feet face backwards and it can also become invisible. Situated in the extreme east, it is a 650 square kilometre area of temperate forests of eastern blue pine and rhododendrons.

The 4,349 square kilometre Jigme Dorji National Park is Bhutan's largest national park, protecting the western parts of Paro, Thimpu and Punakha Dzongkhags and almost the entire Gasa Dzongkhag. Within its confines of subtropical and alpine heights live both lowland farmers and semi-nomadic yak herders.

Several endangered species like the takin, snow leopard, blue sheep, musk deer, red panda and serow live in the park which is also home to leopards, wild dogs, sambar, barking deer, goral, marmot and pika. Over 300 species of birds can also be sighted at this national park.

The 1,023 square kilometre Royal Manas National Park in southern Bhutan is close to the Manas National Park and Manas

Tiger Reserve in the Indian state of Assam. The Indian side of the Manas Park is as enchanting as the Bhutanese. The riverine forests on either side are rich in species of apes, the golden langur, one-horned rhinoceros, hogdeer, wild bear, tiger, elephant and wild buffalo. Also seen are pelicans, peacocks, large cormorants, white-capped red storks and the great pied hornbills.

It was once said that the area around Manas was what the earth looked like before the arrival of man. It is a jewel encrusted land, reflecting Nature's varied and brilliant hues. The river originates in the remote reaches of Bhutan and then rumbles and swirls tumultuously down a rugged mountain valley, past steep cliffs and awesome gorges and fiery rapids.

A Bhutanese wildlife sanctuary till 1966, the Royal Manas National Park was upgraded in 1988. Some of the wildlife in the Bhutanese Manas National Park include rhinoceros, buffalo, tiger, leopard, gaur, bear, elephant and many species of deer. There are some rare species too—the golden langur and the capped langur among them. Ornithologists have recorded over 350 species of birds which include pelicans, peacocks, large cormorants, white-capped red storks and the great pied hornbills.

The Black Mountain National Park spread over 1,723 square kilometres between east and west Bhutan has many virgin forests. Near its southern edge is the Royal Manas National Park. While the entire Himalayan foothills of Nepal and India have been largely cleared of forests, the Black Mountain National Park is still in its natural state with a rich plant and wildlife.

The Phipsoo Wildlife Sanctuary in southern Bhutan, which covers an area of 278 square kilometres, was declared a wildlife sanctuary in 1993 to protect the only remaining natural *sal* forest in Bhutan. Many protected species are found in the sanctuary: axis deer, chital, elephant, gaur, tiger, golden langur and hornbill, to name a few.

The Thrumshing La National Park is a small (768 square kilometres) park between Bumthang and Mongar and is famous for its red panda. It was set up to protect the forests of fir and chir pine.

Spread over an area of 1,300 square kilometres of alpine tundra in eastern Bhutan, next to the Indian state of Arunachal

Pradesh, the Kulong Chhu Wildlife Sanctuary protects the sambar.

In south-eastern Bhutan, a 273 square kilometre area has been set aside as the Khaling/Neoli Wildlife Sanctuary to protect wild elephant, gaur, pygmy hog, hispid hare and other tropical species.

In the western district of Ha where Torsa river enters from Bhutan is situated the 644 square kilometre Torsa reserve which protects the temperate forests.

Bhutan's outdoors are full of beautiful waterfalls

Trekking in Bhutan

...I hurried still more not to miss the vision for which we had come so far. Then the miracle happened. Folded in light mist, hill after hill rolled away into the distance from beneath my feet, and over this green ocean sparkled the vast icebergs of the Himalaya. Never in my remotest dreams had I imagined such beauty could exist on earth... time effaces all memories, but the feelings of that moment are branded in me while I live... looking back today I see more, that it was not only the revelation of my dreams of youth, but the beginning of an experience which has influenced me more than almost any other... the discovery of... a world outside our time.

—Lionel Terry
Conquistadores of the Useless

Trekking in the Himalayas, which was conceived and promoted by the author for the first time on global and commercial basis during the seventies, has caught the imagination of people from all walks of life—artists, writers, poets and scientists. The Himalayas provide unique opportunities for hikers, trekkers, mountaineers, skiers and naturalists.

The Himalayas offer blue or emerald lakes and pine forests, slow-moving rivers and swift mountain streams, rugged rock and snow-covered peaks, grassy downs and meadows resplendent with multicoloured flowers, snow bridges spanning angry torrents, deep and narrow gorges, high passes enveloped in mist, or a mountain peak rising above masses of clouds, reaching out to the deep blue sky. These are sights that the Himalayas alone can offer. No wonder, trekkers and mountaineers look to the Himalayas for fulfilment of their dreams.

It is the grandeur, the beauty and the splendour of the Himalayas that captivates the visitor. The glitter of the morning sun on a snow peak, the majesty of a rugged monolith, the infinite peace of a meadow strewn with daisies, forget-me-nots, buttercups, and wild primulas, the silence of a starry night, the sensuous joy of bathing in the cool waters of a mountain stream are things to be seen and experienced.

Trekking in Bhutan is somewhat different than in other parts of the Himalayas. It is the best way to see and experience the unique rural culture of the Himalayan kingdom. Many treks pass through remote villages and monasteries. In Bhutan porters are not normally available. All personal gears, tents and kitchen items have to be carried by packhorses or, at high altitude, by yaks. Because of the sparse population, one passes through miles and miles of uninhabited and unspoiled terrain. Trekking groups must carry full requirements with them as well as their guides and cooks. Individual trekking is possible in Bhutan but local regulations warrant that all FITs must be accompanied by local guides. Tourism in Bhutan has recently been privatised and there are several tour operators who organise treks.

Bhutan offers some excellent trekking routes through forests, villages and high mountains

Trekkers need to carry backpack with windproof jacket, pullover, camera and water bottle, etc. The Bhutanese crew takes care of all other requirements. They accompany trekkers, set up camps, cook and serve meals. For the first few days they carry fresh vegetables and meat. On long treks one has to depend mostly on tinned food.

Most of Bhutan is covered with dense forests which are rich in flora and fauna. The terrain is usually steeper than in other parts of the Himalayas. There is plenty of wildlife and good opportunities to see a great variety of animals in their native habitats. During the trek you are in true wilderness, with occasional glimpses of snow-clad peaks and forested hills stretching for miles. The climate in Bhutan is much more severe than in Nepal or India. It is windier, damper and colder. There are also frequent changes in weather. The monsoon usually sets in around the middle of June and lasts until the end of September, leaving only a short time for high altitude treks above 4,000 metres.

Bhutan's mountain-trails are still unpolluted and pristine. Several treks pass through rock-terrain. During May-June the profusion of wild flowers, particularly rhododendrons, is spectacular. In Eastern Bhutan, the author saw a riot of colours with rhododendrons stretching for miles on both sides of the entire trek... April-May and mid-September to mid-November are considered the best time for trekking. In the autumn, clear skies and distant views of the mountains are highly rewarding, though temperatures are low. Most of the passes are snow-bound from late November until February.

For trekking in Bhutan, one should be in good physical shape. At times, there are long stretches of steep terrain which can prove exacting, especially in high altitudes. Treks vary from short three-day to long three-week ones. There are several low altitude cultural treks in which anyone can participate. For high altitude treks, one should first spend three or four extra days at around 10,000 feet to acclimatise. Trekking permits are required for all treks. Some of the important treks are briefly described in the following paragraphs.

Dagala Thousand Lakes Trek is a popular trek for visitors

to Thimphu. After half an hour's drive from Thimphu, a seven-day trek starts from Khoma and terminates at Simtokha. The trail passes through terraced paddy fields and coniferous forests with occasional sights of yak. En route, there is the spectacular view of the Dagala range. The trek passes through Utsho lake which is rich in golden trout. The high altitude area near the lake is full of wild alpine flowers. One can spend an extra day or two here to visit numerous lakes in the vicinity.

Druk Path, a six-day trek, starts from Dopshare near Paro and ends at Thimphu. It is a high-altitude trek requiring reasonable fitness. Experienced and strong trekkers can complete this trek in

A trekker looks at the majestic snow covered peaks of the Bhutan Himalayas.

just four days. One can undertake this trek from February to June or September to December. The starting point is the National Museum at Paro. The trail crosses a brook and makes a long gradual climb to a wooded crest. From there, it is a gentle walk along the ridge to a camp site in a yak pasture at 3,450 metres. Thereafter, the trail passes through a thick alpine forest, offering a full view of Jhomolhari and other snow-clad peaks. The trail is rich in rhododendrons. On the third day, one gets an excellent view of the 6,989-metre high Jichu Drake. On the fifth day, if weather permits, one can view Gangkhar Puensum and other adjacent Himalayan peaks.

Jhomolhari Trek is one of the most popular treks starting from Paro. Trekkers take a short ride to the old Drukgyel *dzong* (2,580 metres). The trek starts from here with a short downhill walk on a wide trail. On the very first day, one can have a glimpse of the 7,314-metre high Jhomolhari. There is a spectacular view of the peak from Jangothang. The first three days of the trek are spent in the Paro Chhu valley, passing through paddy fields, a forest of blue pines and apple orchards. The army base at Gunyitsawa in the Jigme Dorji National Park is the last stop before entering Tibet. From here, the trail passes through oaks and ferns, crossing several streams. This is an old invasion and trade route to Phari *dzong* in Tibet. On the fourth day one reaches Jangothang. Nearby is high altitude Tshophu lake. On the fifth day of the trek, one reaches Lingzhi, camping at 4,010 metres. A day's excursion from here takes one to the beautiful lake of Tserim Kang. On the ninth day one reaches Thimphu.

Laya Gasa Trek can be combined with the Jhomolhari Trek. This trek provides a diverse flora and fauna including *takin,* Bhutan's National animal, blue poppy, Bhutan's national flower and blue sheep. One also comes across the Layap people with their unusual culture and the natural hot spring of Gasa. For the first five days the trail follows the route of the Jhomolhari Trek. On the sixth day, one can take a short diversion to the Lingzhi *dzong* which was built in the 17th century and played a vital role in keeping an eye on the invading forces from Tibet. On the eighth day of the trek one reaches Tsheri Jathang where one can have a glimpse of takins which migrate to this valley during the summer months. On the way, Sinche La (5,005 metres) affords a view of the snow-covered peak of Gangchhenta in the north. Two days later reaching Laya, one gets a better view of Gangchhenta as well as Masang Gang (7,165 metres). On the twelfth day, one reaches the Gasa *chorten*, marking the southern boundary of the Jigme Dorji National Park. It will be tempting to spend an extra day at the hot springs of Gasa. The two-week long trek terminates at Tashithang, near Punakha.

Snowman Trek is a very long 23-day trek, taking one to the remote Lunana district. It is considered one of the most difficult treks in the world. Most of the trekkers who take up this challenging trek get themselves insured for emergency evacuation which may become necessary because a heavy snowfall at Lunana can cut one off from the rest of the world. The season for this trek is mid-June to mid-October. The classic snowman trek begins in Paro and follows the Jhomolhari and Laya-Gasa treks as far as Laya. One can shorten it by starting in Punakha and trekking north up the Mo Chhu, following the Laya Gasa trek in reverse. The classic trek, starting from the Drukgyal *dzong*, covers Lingzhi, Laya, Rodophu near the Lunana trail junction, Narethang, Tarina, Woche, Lhedi, Thanza, Tshochena, Jichu Dramo, Chukarpo, Thampe Tsho, Maurothong and Sephu. At Bey and Jichu Dramo one has to cross the 5,140-metre high Rincheu Zoe La.

Gangte Trek is a short three day trek passing through several remote villages. It is especially enjoyable in April when the rhododendrons are in full bloom. The trail winds gently through the forest of firs, oak, spruce, dwarf rhododendron, miniature azaleas, cypress and juniper.

Bumthang Cultural Trek is extremely popular, affording opportunities to visit several villages and Lhakhangs in the central part of Bhutan. This is the best option for the average trekker since the altitude does not go over 3,400 metres. The trek crosses several villages, providing an excellent opportunity to observe the rural life of Bhutan. En route, one can visit Toktu Zampa, Lhakhang, Tahung and Mesitang. The best time for trekking is March to May and again September to November. Soon after passing through Kurjey Lhakhang, one reaches Duer Chhu where one can see the carved Buddha on a rock. One can take a side trip to Ugyen Chholing where there is a lovely palace on top of the hill, built in the traditional Bhutanese design.

Duer Hot Spring Trek, lasting seven days, is recommended for nature lovers. The trek passes through a forest of juniper, spruce, hemlock and maple, attaining a maximum altitude of 4,224 metres. During winter, snow covers the entire area. March to April and September to November are ideal months for this trek. On the fourth day, the trail takes you to a small lake beyond which lies Luli La (4,700 metres), the rocky saddle affording a good view of the mountain. There is the possibility of spotting musk deer, Himalayan boar and blue sheep. Near Duer, a hot spring is situated at 3,590 metres.

Rodang La Trek takes 10 days from Toktu Zampa, passing through Ugyen Chholing, Phokpey, Pemi, Khaine Lhakhang, Tangmachu, Menji, Pemi and Taupang, and terminating at Trashi Yangtse. On the fourth day, one crosses the Rodang La (4,160 metres). On the fifth day, the trail passes below the settlement of the Gomdas who speak the Kurtepa language. A Tibetan-style Umling Mani at 2,180 metres is reached on the sixth day of the trek. It was built by a Tibetan lama.

Dong La, 3,900 metres, which is reached on the ninth day, provides views of high mountains. After reaching the *dzong*, the trail passes through Kulong Chhu. The famous Trashi Yangtse lies three kilometres beyond.

Samtengang Winter Trek is ideal for beginners, lasting as it does only four days. Because of the low altitude one can undertake this trek throughout winter. Starting from Punakha, it passes through Limukha, Chhungsakha and Samtengang. On the last day, after reaching Chhuzomsa, one can go to Wangdue Phodrang by car.

The author, who trekked extensively throughout Bhutan, found a four-day trek from Bumthang to Lhuntse extremely enjoyable. On this trek one gets a beautiful view of the fascinating Tang Valley. A dense rhododendron forest covers the entire route. Near Ungar, there are plenty of oak and magnolia trees, besides rhododendron. At Ungar, there is a saying 'whether you are a king or a pauper, you will have to climb up Rudung La on foot. It is too steep here to ride a horse.'

Another interesting trek for the author was from Trashigang to Merak. This is a four-day trek, passing through Rangjung, Radi, Ngakchung La (3,658 metres) and Jhongkhar. On the second day while passing through the village Thoma, one enters a thick rhododendron forest where the profusion of flowers—white, light pink, pink and red—is unbelievable. The entire trek is long trail of beautiful rhododendrons. The people in this area are very religious and look contented. Prayer flags can be seen all along the trail. The river Nyera Amari provides an excellent setting for camp. The villagers in this area wear yak-wool caps which protect against cold as well as rain. The upper layer of their clothing is of yak or another animal skin which can be suitable in all weather conditions. Except for salt and, perhaps, Bhutanese tea, they appear to be absolutely self-sufficient. The people here are darker in complexion than other Bhutanese. At Merak, which is close to the Indian State of Arunachal Pradesh, one gets fascinating views of the high ridges, forming a natural border. One also gets good views of the snow-clad mountain in the north. For flowers lovers, this is perhaps the best trek in the Himalayas with rhododendrons all along the trail. On the last day of the trek, the trail passes through the tented village of Rangjung where dancing seems to be a passion with local men and women.

The Bhutan Himalayas

According to the general description of the Himalayas, the Bhutan ranges form the Western part of the Assam Himalayas. In the mountaineering literature available, very little is known of the high peaks of Bhutan. Most of the peaks in Bhutan were un-named, and even those named were spelled differently in different publications. With the assistance of Bhutan Tourism Corporation, the author has prepared a comprehensive list of mountain peaks and had given them the most acceptable spellings.

Unlike many other parts of the Himalayas, no detailed survey records of the Bhutan Himalayas are available except description of a few places visited by officers on political or military missions in the past and by a few expeditions who were permitted into Bhutan. Having remained closed to the outside world for centuries Bhutan Himalayas are still regarded as an exclusive, mysterious and rare destination about which the average trekker or climber has heard but little. The great Trigonometrical Survey of the Himalayas during 1845-1868 did not cover Bhutan. Even the individual accounts of exploration are few and rare. One old account of early observations was that of F. Williamson, the Political Officer in Sikkim, in 1933. He travelled from Paro to Bumthang, and then ascended the Chamkhar Chu northwards, crossing Mon La and Kar Chung La (5,316 metres) from where he had a close view of Kula Kangri (7,544 metres). Bhutan is a rugged mountainous land. Thick forests grow on the rain drenched slopes of the mountains.

During the author's first visit along the mountain areas in 1984, it was found that, except Jhomolhari, all other peaks required detailed ground survey with patience. At the time of the visit only Jitchu Drake (6,793 metres) in the Jhomolhari group in western Bhutan was thrown open to the mountaineers. Bhutan Himalayas comprise about 18 peaks over 7,000 metres. Most of these are extremely difficult and dangerous to climb, and thus provide great challenge to mountaineers. Each peak is likely to defy a few attempts before yielding.

The Royal Government of Bhutan opened their doors to foreign expeditions, strictly on commercial basis, only in 1983.

Prior to this only a handful of teams on very special considerations, notably Spencer Chapman's team in 1937 and the joint Indian and Bhutan Armies team in 1970. During 1984, two more peaks, Khang Bum (6,500 metres) and Namshila (6,590 metres) were opened. The two highest peaks in Bhutan were Gangkar Puensum (7,541 metres) and Kula Kangri (7,554 metres). To limit the number of foreign expeditions, the fees for mountaineering expeditions were kept very high. Besides, daily charges, a royalty fee ranging from US $1,000 to 5,000 was also charged, depending on the height and whether the peak was virgin or scaled.

Jhomolhari is a mountain sacred to both Bhutanese and Tibetans and stood on the boundary as a sentinel. On the western slopes of Jhomolhari lay the Chumbi valley which, through the

Bhutan has some of the most challenging peaks, many of them yet unclimbed.

easy Tank La (4,639 metre), provided the main route to Gyantse and Lhasa in Tibet used by the Younghusband Mission in 1903 and by the successive Everest expeditions between the two world wars.

In 1983, an all-women team from Japan, led by Junko Tabei attempted Jitchu Drake. They had intended to climb the east ridge of Jitchu Drake (previously incorrectly identified) as Tsherim-Kang). They set out from Paro on April 21 and travelled through Shana, Soithangthanka and Jangothang to Base Camp located near a beautiful lake at 14,100 feet, on April 30. They made Camps I, II and III at 4,602, 5,105 and 5,197 metres on May 1, 3 and 10 respectively. Above, the route was so steep and difficult that they gave up the attempt on May 14. Fortunately they were given permission to climb Sepchu Kang (5200 metres) near Shodo. On May 20 and 21 nine Japanese and four Bhutanese reached the summit.

The same year Jitchu Drake was attempted by a Austrian team led by Edward Ratheiser. This team attempted the south-west ridge. They placed Base Camp at 4,298 metres and Camp I at the foot of the ridge at 4,800 metres. From there it was a hard climb, chopping steps in the ice and climbing UIAA Grade–IV rock to reach Camp II at 5,600 metres. The ice above Camp II on the knife-edged ridge, which was up to 70 degree, was the most difficult part of the climb. Finally, on May 15, after eight days, at 6,096 metres, they could set up a tiny tent on an ice ledge hacked on the crest of the exposed ridge as Camp III. As time was running out and because of lack of tent space, Werne Sucher, Albert Egger and Alois Stuckler bivouacked at 6,500 metres. These three, together with Sepp Mayerl and Toni Ponholzer, who had climbed from Camp III, reached the summit on May 17 in bad weather.

In 1984, Jitchu Drake was climbed by five members of the Himalayan Association of Japan. The team consisted of Ataru Deguchi, Noboru Sudo, Keiichi Sudo, Masahiko Chigara, Takuo Kikuchi, Kenzo Shinmazu, Moriya Hara, Shoji Seki, led by Kuniaki Yagiharar. They made Base Camp on May 4, 1984 at 4,500 metres by a glacial lake east of the east ridge of Jitchu Drake. They avoided the east ridge where the Japanese women had failed in

1983. They cut short to ascend to a col at 5,300, metres on the east ridge and set up Camp I on May 7. Camp II at 5,600 metres was placed on the 13th. On May 20, K. Sudo Hara, Deguchi and Shinmasu reached the summit (6,790 metres).

Kula Kangri Range is separated from the Eastern Himalaya by the deep valley of the Kuru Chu in the east. It extends west to the Gonto La, the Gophu La and the Mangde Chu. In the eastern portion, several 6,000-metre peaks lie on the Bhutanese-Tibetan frontier, the highest of which is Chura Kang (6,500 metres), just east of the Monlakarchung La. Farther west lie the highest peaks on the Bhutanese Himalaya, mostly on the frontier. The peak which may be the highest, Kula Kangri (7,554 metres) lies north of the main ridge in Tibet. Along the frontier from east to west lie

Below:
Jitchu Drake peak

137

Melunghi Gang (or Kong) (7,000 metres), Gangkar Puensum (7,541 metres) and Chumhari Kang (7,000 metres). Since the surveying has not been very accurate, it might be that Gangkar Puensum, given as 13 metres lower, could be higher than Kula Kangri.

Lunala range extending from the Gonto La, the easternmost source of the Pho Chu on the east, goes in the west to the Toma La where the Mo Chu springs (known downstream as the Tsa Chu and Sankosh). The principal frontier peaks from east to west are Zogophu Gang (7,000 metres), Kangphu Gang (7,200 metres), Jeje Kangphu Kang (7,300 metres) and Teri Kang (7,000 metres). South of the Waghye La and southwest of Teri Kang, entirely within Bhutan, lies Tsenda Gang (7,100 metres).

Starting from the Toma La and the Mo Chu on the east, this range runs from north-east to southwest along the north-western border of Bhutan to the Tremo La. The western edge runs along the river known in Tibet as the Kangphu, in Bhutan as the Amo Chu and in Indian as the Torsa. In the north-east lies Masang Kang (7,200 metres) south of the Toma La. The Kancheda group lies along the frontier. There are three principal summit, the highest of which is 6,678 metres. Farther southwest along the frontier lie Chum Kang (6,536 metres), Tshering Kang (6,800 metres) and Jhomolhari (7,315 metres).

The Academic Alpine Club of Chiba University which had succeeded in the first ascent of Namshila (6,500 metres) in 1985 and Tsenda Gang (7,100 metres) in 1991, explored the Teri Kang area in Lunala in 2001. This team received permission for high altitude trekking as climbing of the peaks in the area of Teri Kang and its vicinity is still closed to foreigners. The area is a part of a course called Snowman-Trek and visited mainly by European trekkers. Though a trekking route, the area is surrounded by mountain ridges having such high passes exceeding 5,000 metres as the Gofu La (5,300 metres), the Gonjyu La (5,100 metres) and the Karakachu La (5,050 metres), and therefore is hardly accessible, particularly in the snow season.

Climbing route is along the right side of the Tarina Chu and traces the side moraine to ascend the Tarina Glacier. The route is mostly covered by impassable rhododendrons. At the Tarina

Glacier end there are two large glacier lakes, and the end of the glacier tongue forms a sheer cliff of 20-30 metres hight. A stream about 10 metres wide drains water of the lakes and the debouchment seems to be resistent enough against erosion.

Lunana is located near the border with China where many fascinating peaks such as Gangka Puensum still remain unclimbed.

Gangkar Puensum (7,541 metres) was attempted by a team led by Philip R Trimble. They approached the peak by going up the Chamkar Chu, a river system draining a cirque 10 to 15 kilometres east of the main peak. They departed from Jakar on September 12 reaching Tsampey on September 15 where they spent five days reconnoitring the Chamkar Chu Glacier. The main party, Yvon Chouinard, Dan Emmett, Frank Morgan, Rick Ridgeway, John Roskelley and Dough Tompkins, arrived at Tsampey on September 23 and continued to explore the area. They satisfied themselves that there was no pass leading from their location to the Mengde Chu, from where they could have approached Gangkar Puensum. From September 30 to October 5 they climbed a number of small peaks of 5,486 to 5,943 metres east of the Chamkar Chu Glacier.

The same year the peak was attempted by the Himalayan Association of Japan. The team was composed of Michifumi Ohuchi, leader, Yoshio Ogata, climbing leader, Hitoshi Watanabe, Sadao Hangaya, Koichi Ezaki, Shinya Kobayashi, Makoto Miyoshi, Tetsuya Kudo, Fumie Kumeda and Shunji Nudeshima. They left Thimphu on August 19 and reached Base Camp on the 31st. They chose the central (south) ridge and established Camp I at 5,220 metres on September 12. But from there the upper part of the ridge looked very difficult. They then tried the west ridge but that proved no better. They returned to the central ridge. They climbed over a snow dome (6,450 metres) on September 22. There were two steep steps before they placed Camp III at 6,880 metres on September 30. On October 1, Kudo came down with pulmonary oedema at Camp II. All members were needed to carry him down. They then decided to give up the route as too dangerous.

Masang Kang (7,200 metres) was attempted in 1985 by a

team from the Kyoto University. They left Thimphu and got to Base Camp at 4,900 metres. They established Advance Base at 5,200 metres. Sohtaro Yokoyama, Goro Hitami, Shigeki Nakayama and Toshihiro Tsukihara climbed to the summit via the northeast spur.

The main group of the expedition left Thimpu on August 30, 1985, and on September 13 got to Base Camp at 5,025 metres on a yak pasture called Dreteng three kilometres southeast of the Toma La. Advance Base was established on September 16 two kilometres west at 5,400 metres. From there the route up the mountain went south. On September 23 they set up Camp I at 6,075 metres below the foresummit. There was steep snow-and-ice climbing before they set up Camp II on the top of the foresummit at 6,417 metres on October 8. Camp III was established on October 12 between the foresummit and the main summit. They measured altitudes which seem to differ from those previously given and believe the summit was about 6,800 metres. On October 13, 1985 the summit was reached by Goro Hitomi, Toshihiro Tsukihara, Kataro Yokoyama and Shigeki Nakayama. On October 14 Dr. Kozo Matsubayashi, Hironori Ito, Shinya Takeda and Masanaru Takai and on October 15 Yasuhiko Kamizomo, Hironori Ito, Koichi Nanno and Tadao Okada repeated the ascent.

In 1986, another Austrian expedition, led by Sepp Mayerl, attempted Gangkar Puensum. The team consisted of Albert Fellinger, Dr. Wolfgang Trost, Gerhard Berger, Toni Ponholzer, Helmut Ortner, Sebastian Ruckensteiner. They left Bumthang on July 28 and took ten days on the approach. Base Camp and Advance Base were at 5,000 and 5,400 metres. They tried the same route as the Japanese in 1985 on the south ridge. They placed Camp I at 6,300 metres at the foot of the ice dome, a prominent summit in the ice ridge. They continued along the sawtooth ice ridge without gaining altitude to the place where the summit ridge shoots sharply up. There, at 6600 metres, they gave up on August 26. There were only two days of clear weather out of the 21 on the mountain. Daily snowfall was up to 50 cms. They had a terrible time on the mountain with continuous danger of avalanches.

In 1986, Gangkar Puensum was also attempted by a team

of five Britons, an American and a New Zealander, led by Steve Barry. They took ten days to reach Base Camp at 5,181 metres in continuous rain and sleet. They crossed the Mangde Chu Glacier moraines to Advance Base at the foot of the mountain. Camp I at 6,248 metres was on a ridge at the head of a gully, a single tent at a precarious angle. Wind confined climbers there for two days before they descended to Advance Base. After a break in the weather, they returned to Camp I and set up Camp II at 6,553 metres. After reaching 6,858 metres, they were repulsed by strong winds. Food was running out as yaks could not reach Base Camp in deep snow. At the request of the Bhutanese government, Indian Army helicopters dropped food. Finally the members were airlifted to Paro.

First ascent to the main peak of Jitchu Drake was finally accomplished by the legendary British climber, Douglas Scot in 1989. According to his account published in the American Alpine Journal 1989, he states:

> After an unsuccessful attempt on the south-east ridge by Japanese ladies in the pre-monsoon season of 1983, Austrians climbed to the lower south summit by the south-west ridge but again went only to the south summit (American Alpine Journal, 1986, page 210). During the autumn, an Italian expedition attempted this elegant line, but tragically two climbers were hurled down the east face when the crest of the ridge broke away (AAJ, 1985, pages 244-246). On May 5, our group arrived at Thangothang. Our camp obviously made a good base for exploring the western side of Jitchu Drake. Even though the mountain is only 22,277 feet high, we would still have to acclimatise during the next two weeks and that is what we did, first on the west, then on the east and finally on the south of the mountain. On one long day on May 7, we moved up the moraine of the South Jitchu Drake Glacier to where it merged with icefields coming down from the western side. We could see only two-thirds of the western ribs reaching up into the clouds. Although the reconnaissance was inconclusive, we moved camp to check out the east side. The day before departure, Victor Saunders severely strained

his ankle, but he set off with us, riding a horse. We eventually set up camp at 14,000 feet on a beautiful oval lake below the east side. During the next week, we pitched a camp on the rocky ridge that separates the two glaciers that come down from the east face of Jitchu Drake. It looked steep, seeing it head on, and dangerous with huge mushrooms of snow barring the way at several places. The only possibility seemed to be up the south face. We established Advance Base on a lovely lake nestling in the rocks at 16,000 feet. Whilst the rest of us brought up more supplies, Neil Lindsay and Lindsey Griffin carried out a superb reconnaissance of the approaches to the south face and reached a point just below the plateau and most of the way through the icefall that tumbles down towards the South Jitchu Drake Glacier. A few days later, we established Camp I at 18,000 feet on the great ice shelf. We retreated to Base Camp for a rest before the actual climb. On May 24, we left Base Camp for Advance Base. Saunders was hobbling on his ankle, Griffin had a torn shoulder muscle, Sharu Prabhu had stomach trouble and I was trying to combat old age. Only David Rose was fit, but he was on his first Himalayan expedition as a reporter for the Guardian. Sharu Prabhu was an Indian who had climbed to 24,000 feet with the Indian expedition to Everest in 1984 and she had been to 25,000 feet with us on our north-east-ridge Everest expedition. Neil Lindsay had to leave for home. On May 26, we broke trail in sweltering heat to the base of the south face and traversed a mile in dense fog. We had to find a camp site nearby. In the morning, we set out rather late and saw we had no hope for reaching the only likely bivouac site some 2,000 feet higher. We settled for leading out and leaving our four ropes for the morrow. Back in the tents, by one o'clock we were hammered by the usual afternoon storm. On May 28, we were away by 4:30, moved rapidly up to the bergschrund and up the four rope-lengths. The next pitch was steep with a vertical step of hard green ice. At one o'clock, Saunders expressed doubts about continuing, but I suggested we should take a diagonal line for the south-east ridge and a possible bivouac site. By the eighth pitch, the storm was very violent and the snow was pouring down the face in waves. We were still two pitches from the south-east ridge. Just as the sun was setting, Saunders reached the ridge. I led up the heavily corniced ridge for 100 metres to a flat part of the cornice, where we hacked out space for our bivy tents. The next morning, Saunders and I found a better camp site some 500 feet higher, protected by a steep bulge in the ridge. Later that day, we all moved up, occupying what was probably the final Japanese camp, having joined their route on the ridge. Graffin had not been sleeping well and Rose felt that we three others could make faster progress if he stayed with Graffin. Sharu Prabhu, Victor Saunders and I were off at 2:30 on May 30. From time to time we came across Japanese rope. The twelfth pitch took us to the south summit, where we found the end of the Japanese line. We still had to descend 100 feet on the corniced ridge and climb 1000 feet of easy snow slopes on the west side of the higher north summit. By midday we were on the summit (6,790 metres, 22,277 feet). We had to concentrate all our thoughts on the tricky descent, making one awkward, often diagonal abseil after another to arrive in Camp IV just before dark. The next day, after down-climbing two pitches and abseiling twelve full rope-lengths, we were back on the glacier.

In October 1991, Peter Mould led a combined climbing trekking expedition to north-west Bhutan (Basingthang Peaks) which had permission to tackle unclimbed "trekking Peaks" up to 5,700 metres from a Base Camp at 4,200 metres on Basingthang yak pasture, 12 miles south-east of Jomolhari. On October 12, they climbed climbed P 5,640 (5,040 metres) in the Ngum Tang Gang group from a camp at 4,800 metres near the top of the Riburi Ridge. The peak lies 2/1/2 miles west-north-west of Base Camp. A satisfying steep ridge of snow and ice led to an airy summit. There are two more unclimbed peaks in this group. On October 15, they climbed P 5,487 (5,487 metres). The north summit of this easy saddle-shaped peak was visible from Base with two small rocky summits of 5,487 and 5,450 metres at either end. On October 16, climbed both summits in ten and a half hour round-trip from Base. On October 15, Wohney Gang (5,589 metres) was climbed in a 12-hour round-trip from a camp 100 metres below the 4,969-metres Wohney La to the north of the peak.

The same year, a Dutch team, led by Ronald Naar, organised a climbing expedition to Western Bhutan. Their first objective was a mountain that the Swiss trekking map of Bhutan calls Chatarake and is given as 6,500 metres high. This is also called Djodrake by locals. From Paro they trekked via Drukgyal Dzong into a region probably not previously visited by Westerners. On October 27, they reached the foot of the north-east buttress on a 4,800-metre pass. They climbed the next day to the summit, which they reached at 1:10 P.M. the height was a little disappointing, in reality "only" 5,570 metres. From there they travelled to the region just previously visited by the British party, the Basingthang peaks. The British had suggested that there was a hidden "Andean-type" mountain which was probably the highest in the Wohney-Gang group. After heading up several wrong valleys they finally found the "Andean" mountain. On November 5, they reached a crevassed glacier and got to the summit of the peak (5,780 metres). However, it was not the highest of the group. This proved to be a sharp rock needle, further south. After traversing a narrow ice ridge, they climbed to its summit. From there, they headed for Kang Bum, given on maps as 6,494 metres. However, the mountain looks lower although certainly more than 6,000 metres. They crossed into and ascended the Thimpu valley. Their horse driver, who had accompanied the Japanese first-ascent party, explained the route. On November 9, they were camped on Kang Bum's southern glacier. In order to reach the upper glacier, they had to climb threatened slopes and both steep rock and ice. On November 11, they left their Camp II before sunrise. After a steep section to a foresummit, they climbed on over several false summits to the summit at nine A.M. where they had a magnificent view all the way from Everest and Kanchenjunga to the 7,000-metre peaks of the Lunana district to the east. They were back in Thimpu, the Bhutanese capital, on November 14.

In October 1991, a Japanese team from Chiba University Alpine Club, led by Fumitaka Sakurai attempted, also known as Tsenda Gang. The height of the peak has been described as 7,000 metres, but the Japanese team found it much less. The team consisted of Hiroshi Kodama, Kosuke Honma, Ryoji Takahashi, Takeharu Shumiya. After an approach from Thimpu, which began on October 12, they arrived at Base Camp at 4,700 metres on October 20 on the south side of Tsendakang. They fixed rope up to 5,300 metres in the icefall for two days, but were stopped by crevasses. They changed to the west side and made Advance Base under the south-west face to Tsendakang at 5,350 metres on October 28. To get there took five hours, which included crossing a 5,100-metre pass. From Advance Base, they climbed a couloir threatened by rockfall to reach the west ridge. They continued up the snow ridge, fixing 750 metres of rope to the base of a steep rotten-rock step. After leaving supplies, they returned to Advance Base. At 8:30 A.M. on November 6, Kodama, Honma and Sakuria started from Advance Base, climbed to the top of the fixed ropes and another 150 metres of rock. They continued up the steep ridge on unstable snow. As night fell, there was no place to camp. They bivouacked at 9:30 P.M. on the snow face at 5,950 metres. The next day, they continued along the ridge until they found a flat spot for Camp II. At 6:40 A.M. on November 8, they headed for the summit. There was first a 180-metre-high icefall. They kept on along the slope to the summit wall. In three pitches they got to a shoulder below the top and climbed three more pitches to the summit, which they reached at one P.M., my altimeter indicating 6,310 metres), although the official altitude was given as 7,200 metres. They found it certainly much lower than 7,000 metres.

A team consisting of three Brotons—John Lecky, Sean Smith and Julian Freeman Attwood and two Americans—Steve Sustad and Ed Webster, attempted Masagang in 1993, by a new route. They flew to Paro on April 5, spent the 6th sorting food and gear in Thimphu and drove to the roadhead on the Mo Chu some miles up from Panakha Dzong on the 7th. With 30 ponies, they walked via Damji, Gaza Dong, Koina to Laya from April 8 to 11. At Laya they changed to yaks and did a short day up valley to the east of

Masagang. They realised they were being taken to the Base Camp from which the Japanese in 1985 had made the first ascent. They decided to double back to the south-west via Laya. After reaching the south-west valley, two days of reconnaissance convinced them that the route would not go for their party. They therefore decided to return with all yaks to the eastern valley between Masagang and Tsenda Kang. They could see no feasible routes on the east side of the mountain and so had to set up Base Camp at 4,500 metres at the old Japanese camp and attempt their route. On April 21 they established the site of Advance Base at 5,000 metres. They placed Camp I at 5,600 metres on April 26, having headed north to the Tibetan border to avoid the main Masagang Glacier icefall. On April 27, they got to the col at 6,000 metres with magnificent views. On May 2, they established Camp II at 6,150 metres near an ice pyramid below the forepeak. The weather continued to be bad. On May 14, Webster, Smith and Sustad reconnoitered 200 metres above Camp II but reported the route would not go. They found a hard traverse of 500 metres under massive, overhanging, unstable ice towers. There simply was no other feasible route onto the easy upper slopes and we had to admit defeat.

For the mountaineering enthusiasts, I have prepared the following list from available records with the assistance of several Bhutan officials. All peaks except the Jhomolhari Group require detailed ground survey verification. All heights appear approximate, and a few of the marked peaks may actually not exist!

S. No.	Name	Height in metres	Group	In some maps shown as
1.	Jhomolhari	7,315	Jhomolhari	Chomolhari
2.	Jhomolhari II (Local name Jomo)	6,935	Jhomolhari	-
3.	Jitchu Drake	6,793	Jhomolhari	
4.	Tserim Gang	6,532	Jhomolhari	Takaphu
5.	Gieu Gang	7,200	Jhomolhari	Gyu Kang
6.	Khang Bum	6,500	Jhomolhari	-
7.	Tseja Gang	6,833	Laya	Tseja Kang
8.	Unnamed	6,678	Laya	-
9.	Gangchen Tag	7,000	Laya	Kancheta
10.	Matsa Gang	7,200	Laya	Masa Gang
11.	Tsenda Gang	7,000	Lunana	-
12.	Gang Chhen	7,200	Lunana	Kang Chem
13.	Tsenda Gong	7,100	Lunana	-
14.	Teri Kang	7,000	Lunana	-
15.	Jeje Kangphu	7,300	Lunana	-
16.	Kangphu Gang	7,200	Lunana	Kangphu Kang
17.	Table Mountain (Zogophu Gang)	7,000	Lunana	Zongophu Kang
18.	Jhomolhari Gang	7,000	Lunana	Chomolhari Gang
19.	Namshila	6,595	Lunana	-
20.	Kula Kangri	7,554	Bumthang	-
21.	Chumhari Gang	7,000	Bumthang	-
22.	Gangkar Puensum	7,541	Bumthang	-
23.	Unnamed	7,239	Bumthang	-
24.	Melunghi Gang	7,000	Bumthang	Melunghi Kang
25.	Chura Gang	7,000	Bumthang	-
26.	Unnamed	6,389	Trashigang	-
27.	Unnamed	6,270	Trashigang	-

For all those who wish to plan a climbing expedition in Bhutan, it is advisable to get in touch with the government to find out the latest rules and regulations concerning permission and royalties for various peaks.